IN PRAISE
OF
PUBLIC LIFE

☐

Joseph I. Lieberman

with Michael D'Orso

A Touchstone Book
Published by SIMON & SCHUSTER
NEW YORK • LONDON • TORONTO • SYDNEY • SINGAPORE

SIMON & SCHUSTER
Rockefeller Center
1230 Avenue of the Americas
New York, NY 10020

Copyright © 2000 by Joseph I. Lieberman
All rights reserved,
including the right of reproduction
in whole or in part in any form.
SIMON & SCHUSTER and colophon are
registered trademarks of Simon & Schuster, Inc.
Designed by Edith Fowler
Manufactured in the United States of America

10   9   8   7   6   5   4   3   2

Library of Congress Cataloging-in-Publication Data

Lieberman, Joseph I.
    In praise of public life / Joseph I. Lieberman with Michael D'Orso.
        p. cm.
    Includes index.
        1. Lieberman, Joseph I.   2. Legislators—United States—
Biography.   3. United States. Congress. Senate—Biography.
4. United States—Politics and government—1989–
5. Connecticut—Politics and government—1951–   I. D'Orso,
Michael.   II. Title.
E840.8.L46 A3 2000
328.73'092—dc21
[B]   99-059278
ISBN 0-684-86774-5

for

HADASSAH FREILICH LIEBERMAN

CONTENTS

PROLOGUE

THERE ARE TIMES, now and then, when my mother will read something critical about me in the newspapers, or she'll hear the fatigue in my voice during an evening phone conversation from my home in Washington to hers in Connecticut. "Sweetheart," she'll say, in that voice I've heard all my life, "do you really *need* this?"

I laugh and answer, "Yes, Mom, I really do need this. I love it."

Of course, my mother knows what my answer will be, and I know she is proud of it. But her question makes a good point. There's a lot you have to learn to live with if you are going to hold elected office and live a public life in America today. Privacy, for example, is difficult to maintain, for you and your family. Criticism, when you receive it (and you can count on receiving it, from political adversaries, if not from the man on the street or from the media), is sometimes searing, frequently personal and almost always public. The media—newspapers, television, radio—shadow public officials' every move, analyzing their words and deeds, scrutinizing their intentions, second-guessing their decisions and questioning their intelligence, not to mention their integrity. In this age of around-the-clock live cable television news,

radio and the Internet, those judgments are instantly and
constantly transmitted, day in and day out, to tens of millions
of viewers, listeners and readers, often without adhering
to the traditional journalistic standards of accuracy and relia-
bility.

It's hard to imagine a career—other than professional
athletics or entertainment—where one's job performance is
as visible, as studied and as magnified as a politician's. Like
an athlete and an entertainer, an elected official today must
face questions not only about how he is doing his job but
how he is living his life—and how he has *lived* his life. Besides being expected to account for almost any aspect of his
present existence, he may well be asked to explain things he
did years or even decades ago, long before he entered public
life. Unlike an athlete and an entertainer, whose wayward behavior—past or present—can often embellish a career, a
politician's words and deeds are typically held to the highest
of standards, and he is, in the most acutely direct sense, answerable for those actions—answerable to the public. They
are the people who hired him. They are the people who can
fire him. And they are also the people to whom he must constantly turn for not only approval but also tangible support.

If you are going to live the life of a politician, you have
to learn to ask people for support—political and financial.
That is not always easy or comfortable. You have to ask them
as well for their votes. And you have to be aware that they
might want something in return that you may not be able to
give them, which they may not understand, and which they
may therefore resent.

As a politician, you will also have to endure the disdain
of those who consider your profession little more than bartering political favors for money and votes. You may well

be sullied by the fight for election, drawn into the kind of negative campaigning and mudslinging that leaves both winners and losers dirtied and degraded in the public eye. Upon entering office, you will step into yet another arena that has turned uglier than ever before, this one infected with the partisan infighting of political parties that are polarized today to a degree unequaled in our nation's recent history.

So why in the world would anyone in his or her right mind choose such a life?

Well, I'm afraid fewer and fewer people *are* choosing it. This is bad for our democracy, and it is also the reason I am writing this book.

I had lunch not long ago with a group of interns in my Senate office. I try to do this each summer, at the end of these students' time with us, as a way of thanking them and saying goodbye before they head back to their colleges. This particular group came from a broad mix of campuses, including UCLA, the University of Virginia, Trinity College, the College of William and Mary, and my alma mater, Yale. Toward the end of the meal, I asked how many of them were thinking about pursuing a career in public life after graduation. Most were, which was not surprising. They probably wouldn't have spent their summer on Capitol Hill if they weren't. But when I went further and asked how many of their friends and classmates were considering a career in politics, they said not many, if any. I asked why.

"They think," said one, "that politics is just a lot of noise and not much is accomplished."

"It's too partisan," said another. "And too nasty. And politicians don't have any privacy."

"Too often," said a third, "it seems like politicians spend most of their time raising money—big money."

Meanness. Big money. Partisanship.

Not much accomplished.

The reasons these students ticked off for their classmates' aversion mirror the disdain most of the nation feels
right now for politics and for politicians.

That is not surprising when you think about the sordid
spectacle that culminated in the impeachment trial of President Bill Clinton, the partisan bickering and bloodletting
unleashed throughout that national crisis, the aura of zealous
pursuit infecting the independent counsel's investigation, the
media's seemingly unquenchable thirst for scandal, the as-
cent of a character like Larry Flynt as a moral arbiter and influence on this momentous process. In the wake of such a
gaudy and demeaning saga at what is supposed to be the
highest, most dignified level of our society, is it any wonder
that Americans by the millions simply turned away in disap-
pointment and disgust?

Voter turnout for the November 1998 elections, which
followed the President's nationally televised "confession" of
his relationship with Monica Lewinsky and the subsequent
beginning of the impeachment proceedings in the House,
was 36 percent—the lowest for any midterm election since
1942. Think about that number. For every eligible American
who voted, there were two who did not.

That disheartening statistic tells us that fewer Americans than ever can muster enough trust in their government
to conclude that it is worth voting. This cynicism has infected the American people to the point where a disturbingly
large number of them no longer believe that public life in
our democracy—the very core of our system of representative government—is worthy of their respect, let alone their
involvement. In a survey taken in 1964, three out of four

Americans said they believed in their government and trusted their elected leaders. A similar survey taken last year found that figure had dropped to one in four.*

One in four.

Public confidence did not plummet overnight. It did not begin with Bill Clinton. Politicians and government have endured suspicion and a certain degree of scorn since the birth of this nation. This skepticism on the part of the American public is a grand tradition, as deeply rooted in our society as the spirit of freedom and independence and limited government. What is new, however, is the degree to which that suspicion and scorn have grown in the past thirty years. These three decades have seen an unprecedented parade of betrayals of the public's trust, from the deception that lay behind the Vietnam War, to the shock of the Watergate scandal, to Iran-Contra and the partisan political and cultural warfare that erupted in the 1980s, to the personal attacks on public figures like Judge Robert Bork, Speaker Jim Wright and Justice Clarence Thomas, to the unseemly revelations of campaign finance wrongdoing in 1996, and on through the earthshaking impeachment experience of 1998 and 1999.

That's an awful beating for a political system to take over the course of just one generation. And it has brought us to a low point in the American people's relationship with their government. They are experiencing a real crisis of confidence not just in politicians but in the value of public life in our democracy, which troubles me deeply because I've lived that life for those same past thirty years—virtually my entire adulthood—and I think it deserves better. I've experienced

* Thomas H. Silver, "The Polling Report," April 22, 1977, p. 1. In Richard Morin and Dan Balz, "Reality Check: The Politics of Mistrust," Washington Post, January 28, 1996, p. A1.

its challenges and satisfactions, and I've felt its pitfalls and
pressures. I know the strains it can put on a personal life—on
a marriage and a family. I've felt the probing eye of the media
push further and further into public officials' offices and
homes. I've seen the role of money in political campaigns
grow more uncontrollable and corrosive year after year. I've
felt the viciousness of partisanship infect the process of politics to the point where reasonable collaboration becomes almost impossible. I've watched good men go bad, their
judgment clouded by zealotry and ideological obligation, by
ego and ambition, by the dark side of power and prestige, or
simply and sadly by desires that become needs.

The American people have watched these things as well.
Every day, on the pages of hundreds of newspapers and magazines, they read ringside accounts of the latest political bat-
tle, or corruption, or scandal. Every day they watch the
constant flow of television news broadcasts. They listen to
analysts on radio talk shows dissect and diagnose the political
news of the day with each other, with the audience and with
the politicians themselves. They scour the Internet. And for
a firsthand look at government doing its business, they watch
C-SPAN.

With such a wealth of access and input, it's easy to feel
that we've got more than enough information about public
life and those who are living it to make conclusive judgments
about the quality, the value and even the future of that life.

But, with all that Americans are shown of public life
through the media, there is more that they do not see that is
good and hopeful. There are aspects of life in goverment that
are not conveyed by today's cameras and tape recorders that
are fascinating, encouraging and even enjoyable. Without
understanding these fuller dimensions of this life, it is hard
to honestly and accurately judge it, or to prescribe solutions

for what ails it. Communicating that more complete picture of public life is exactly what I want to do in this book.

Last year a group called the Council for Excellence in Government sponsored a poll that found that two out of three Americans feel "disconnected" from their government, that more than half our society does not believe the government is any longer "of, by and for the people," and that the segment of our society that feels most estranged from government is the young, ages eighteen to thirty-four.

This is what those interns were trying to tell me at lunch, and this is what chills me most—the prospect of the best of the next generation turning their backs on politics and public life. It is always, of course, the young upon whom the future direction of our society depends, and right now that generation is abandoning its government.

Not that they don't care about society. In fact, while those who are now coming of age in America may feel disconnected from government, they *do* feel a strong connection to their community and its needs, stronger in some ways than the generations that preceded them in the 1970s and 1980s. While they may be shunning political careers, they are turning in growing numbers toward public service— community groups, advocacy groups—and volunteer work. A recent national study of college freshmen shows that more students are choosing schoolteaching as a career than at any time in the past quarter century. Why? Certainly not for ego or pay. No, the reason cited repeatedly by the students in this survey was their desire to "make a difference."*

Of course, we should celebrate the fact that these young people are choosing to turn their talent, vision and hope not

---

*Mary B. W. Tabor, "Despite Low Prestige and Pay, More Answer the Call to Teach," New York Times, July 11, 1999, p. A1.

toward just themselves—as seemed to be prevalent in the
'80s—but toward one another, toward their community, toward those in need.

But it also brings me back to the question I asked at the
beginning: Why in the world would anyone, including the
next generation, choose to live the public life of a politician
today? Why, to repeat my mother's question, do I really need
this?

The answer, I would suggest, is the same one those future teachers gave: to make a difference. For all that is wrong
with our system of government, and there is much that needs
repair, it remains a place where one can truly and uniquely
make a difference, where one can help improve our country
and even, occasionally, the world.

We need to convince more young people who want to
make a difference to enter public life. For the American ex-
periment in self-government to remain vital, we need more
people to serve in that government and to live public lives. If
we didn't have politicians, we would have to invent them. We
can turn our backs and abandon them in disgust, thereby en-
suring that the government does indeed belong to the privileged and powerful few. Or we can conclude that public life
is a worthy pursuit, that it can be an honorable, constructive,
satisfying, enjoyable career, deserving of the best among us.

We need to nurture this belief, especially in the generation now coming of age. We need to restore the trust and
faith that have been so badly damaged. If this sounds as if I'm
talking about a personal or even a marital relationship, it
should. Trust is the foundation of any relationship, and the
first step toward repairing the people's damaged trust in their
government is to establish a foundation of clarity, honesty
and understanding.

It is toward that end that I want to share some of what

PROLOGUE17

I've come to know and understand about public life over the course of my own career. I'd like to give a sense of what it looks and feels like, from the inside, and why I'm so glad I chose it. This book is not an autobiography. But it is personal, because I want to illustrate through my own experiences the nature, complexities, possibilities and satisfactions of public life. I will describe how my public life has affected my private life and vice versa, and ask what lines can be drawn between the two.

I'm still living that life, still learning, still trying to figure out how to deal with and repair the problems that persist. I will take a look at some of those problems in the pages that follow. I will also describe what I believe is right and good about this life, which, in my opinion, far outweighs the bad, because this is a book with a point of view. I write in praise of public life for all who care about the future of our democracy.

In 1976, in the wake of the Watergate scandal, Jimmy Carter came up with a wonderful one-line insight about the relationship between the public and its elected leadership: The American people, he said, deserve a government as good as they are.

Nearly a quarter century later, the American people still deserve as much, and they still do not have it. But my life in politics tells me they are closer to it than they think.

I hope, after reading these pages, that you will agree and decide to do something yourself to make it even better.

1

ON POLITICS
AS A CAREER

THERE IS MUCH TALK these days of the "rampant careerism" that has, in the view of some observers, come to infect our government. The term "professional politician" is pronounced with distaste, the implication being that holding public office cannot be both a calling and a career, that the latter inevitably contaminates the former. Government, from this point of view, has become a wasteful haven for men and women with suspect motives who settle into its recesses for the duration, feeding from the public trough, fattening themselves on power and influence while constantly raising money for reelection and only fitfully producing anything of substance.

The solution? Do away with the "Beltway insiders." Replace them, as Ross Perot once suggested, with "citizen amateurs." Impose term limits to make sure no one hangs around too long.

This scorn of political "careerists" is nothing new. When our nation was created, the Founding Fathers felt strongly that those who hold elected office should do it as a public service, not as a profession, and should rotate in and out of public office after a limited period of time. The men who agreed to govern (they were all men then) had well-

established, successful nonlegislative careers—farming, ship-
ping, commerce—to which they returned once their time in
office was over. George Washington, Thomas Jefferson,
James Madison were "gentlemen" of the upper class, drafted
by their colleagues and contemporaries to offer their skills
and services to their fledgling country. They saw themselves
as public servants, virtually as volunteers. Although they
spent much of their lives in service of their country, it was
considered unseemly to actively *seek* office, and unthinkable
to consider public life your "job."

But it is important to understand that term limits, which
were a feature of the Articles of Confederation, were not included in the Constitution because they didn't work. They
had hobbled the performance of our pre-Constitutional government. Term-limited, part-time lawmakers and governors
at the federal and state levels were either weak or absent.
They literally failed to show up for work because they were
busy elsewhere. By the turn of the nineteenth century, government began to attract a different breed of officeholder,
politicians who actively pursued seats in Congress and, once
they had them, made it clear that they intended to stay. That
brought an entirely different set of risks and advantages. The
Senate, with its six-year terms, its relatively small membership and the prospect of those members' perpetual reelection, became a particularly worrisome place to some. Henry
Clay, writing to his wife in the 1830s, complained that the
Senate was "no longer a place for any decent man. It is
rapidly filling up with blackguards."*

Those sentiments are prevalent today—about the Senate, the House and even the presidency. I don't disagree that

---

* *Quoted in Elizabeth Drew,* The Corruption of American Politics *(New
York: Birch Lane, 1999), p. 26.*

there are, and always have been, legitimate concerns in our society about the character and motivation of the people who choose politics as a career, since we are, after all, human. But to suspect those who make it their career simply *because* they have made it their career, to pronounce them "professionals" as if that were a derogatory term, demeans the important work our society needs professional politicians to do.

To call someone a professional implies that he or she has attained a high level of expertise at what he or she does. We generally respect that. We value it. When we need a plumber, we seek a professional. The same is true with a neurologist, or an architect, or a hairstylist. Why should we ask any less of the people who run our government?

In most cases, in most professions, expertise comes from experience. It is built over time. It is typically attained by working with and learning from other professionals in the same field. This is as true of government as it is of carpentry. What I learned about the complexities of legislation during the ten years I spent as a state senator in Connecticut was invaluable when I became a United States senator. And what I have learned during my eleven years on Capitol Hill makes me a much better senator today than I was when I began.

Of course I'm not saying that our political system should not sometimes be shaken up through the election of a new kind of leader, like Jesse Ventura in our time, or that it should not be open to the fresh perspective of someone from an entirely different profession, a person who has been successful, say, in business, or, as in the case of one of my Senate colleagues, Bill Frist of Tennessee, in medicine. But we would not want to have a Senate composed of one hundred people who had never held public office before. It would not govern well.

Remember, our advanced society operates on the concept of division of labor. The entirely self-sufficient individual in America today is nearly nonexistent. Few of us have the skills needed to raise our own food, build our own houses or mend our own wounds. We are each more or less specialists, experts to one degree or another at what we do, dependent upon other specialists to do what *they* do to take care of our needs. There is, built into this system, a great degree of freedom and comfort. We can rest assured that while we are doing our job, others are doing theirs. The police, for instance. And food inspectors. Air traffic controllers. And, yes, politicians. A friend of mine who is not in government, informing me recently that she was going to the ballet that evening, put it this way: "You're taking care of the government tonight so I don't have to."

That's why the notion of term limits has never made sense to me. It precludes the possibility of a legislator building expertise over time. It denies the value of experience. And it ignores the fact that our political system already includes built-in term limits decided by the voting public every two, or four, or six years—they are called elections.

Where the concept of political careerism truly becomes an issue, it seems to me, is around the question of purpose. It is important, of course, to understand a person's purpose for choosing to enter political life. In almost every case I know of, as a person begins his political career, those intentions are honorable and sincere. But they don't always stay that way. Once people enter this life, they become vulnerable to a host of pressures and forces that can skew their purposes, sometimes without their awareness. It is these forces—partisanship, special interest groups, the need for money, the demands of campaigning, the power of the media—that can twist a politician's priorities and make keeping one's seat become more important than what one does while sitting in it.

That is when the voters should, and usually do, vote the way-ward politician out of office, because that's the way the system cleanses and corrects itself.

Now, I want to share some of my own upbringing with you because that will illustrate what shaped my pur-pose and drew me to politics and public life. I believe that the origins of my interest in politics are similar in theme, if not in details, to those of most people I have known in gov-ernment. I hope that my story will therefore also convey a better understanding of what can move people to careers in public life.

2

THE ROOTS
OF A PUBLIC LIFE

LAST YEAR I attended the thirty-fifth reunion of my Yale college class. At this advanced age, we are apparently supposed to be thinking of transitions in our lives, so the organizers of the reunion asked Gail Sheehy, the author of *Passages*, a book about life's transitions, to speak to us. In preparation for her remarks, Sheehy interviewed several class members about the paths our lives had followed. During the course of our conversation she surprised me by asking, "How do you *relax?*"

And I surprised myself with my answer: "I observe the Sabbath." I went on to mention other things I like to do to relax. Exercise. Travel. Go to the movies when I can. Read, although I never have time to read as much as I'd like. But before anything else, the Sabbath was what came to my mind because that is when I truly rest and relax. I would probably begin to answer the question of how I got into politics through the same surprising portal of my faith because it has so much to do with the way I navigate through each day, personally and professionally. It has provided a foundation, order and purpose to my life.

I was raised in a religiously observant family, which gave me the clear answers of faith to life's most difficult questions.

My parents and my rabbi, Joseph Ehrenkranz, taught me that our lives were a gift from God, the Creator, and with it came a covenantal obligation to serve God with gladness by living as best we could, according to the law and values that God gave Moses on Mount Sinai. The summary of our aspirations was in the Hebrew phrase *tikkun olam*, which is translated "to improve the world," or, "to repair the world," or, more boldly, "to complete the Creation which God began." In any translation, this concept of *tikkun olam* presumes the inherent but unfulfilled goodness of people and requires action for the benefit of the community. It accepts our imperfections and concludes that we, as individuals and as a society, are constantly in the process of improving and becoming complete. Each of us has the opportunity and responsibility to advance that process both within ourselves and the wider world around us. As Rabbi Tarfon says in the Talmud, "The day is short and there is much work to be done. You are not required to complete the work yourself, but you cannot withdraw from it either." These beliefs were a powerful force in my upbringing, and seem even more profound and true to me today.

My faith was just one of many great gifts my father and mother, Henry and Marcia Lieberman, gave to me. They were extraordinarily supportive parents—and superior role models in living according to the principles of integrity, hard work and community service that they preached. I have a clear memory of my dad sitting behind the counter of his liquor store in Stamford, Connecticut, reading literature and philosophy between customers, as classical music drifted from the radio on the shelf behind him. He didn't go to college—he never had that chance—but he was as civilized, cultured and intellectually curious a man as I have ever known. He read the *New York Times* every day. We watched the news on television every night. Because of him, Edward R. Murrow and Walter Cronkite were presences in our family life, as they were in so many American households in the 1950s. In that sense there was an awareness of current events in our home. But our family—my mother, my father, my two sisters, Rietta and Ellen, and my grandmother Minnie, whose home we all shared until I was eight—didn't sit around the dinner table each evening discussing and debating the news of the day. Politics came up now and then in our household, but it wasn't a focus.

My grandmother Minnie, who I called by the Yiddish Baba, was a very strong influence on my early life, in ways that still affect me today and that I now realize helped guide me into public life. Baba, my mother's mother, was a heroic figure to me. Born and raised in Central Europe, widowed with five children while she was in her thirties, Baba was a deeply religious woman and very resilient. She was my window to the Old World and my path to appreciating the New World. I could imagine the Old World through the stories she told me. Baba didn't come to America until she was married and a mother. Before that, she spent her life in a European village where Jews were not, to say the least, always treated kindly. To move from such a place to a small American city where, as she walked to synagogue on a Saturday, her Christian neighbors would pass and say respectfully, "Good Sabbath, Mrs. Manger!" was an endless source of delight and gratitude for her. My grandmother had something with which to compare her life in America. She never took her freedom and opportunity here for granted, and she made sure I didn't either. Baba also set a standard for service in our family, as one of the founders of the Hebrew Ladies Educational League in Stamford, a classic immigrant, self-help, pre-welfare organization which raised money and gave it quietly to those who needed it for food or clothing or birth or burial.

We may not have been a particularly political family, but we were a patriotic one, beginning with my grandmother and continuing with my father, who had served proudly in World War II. I was raised to love my country. I remember my dad saying to me once when I was a teenager that he had no complaint whatsoever about writing the check to pay his taxes to the government because he appreciated the opportunities this country was giving him and his family. I have to say that Dad's attitude shifted a bit toward the end of his life, when he began to feel that some of his tax money was being wasted. But even then, he still wrote his checks to the IRS with gratitude and without complaint.

My first purely political memories are of watching the televised Kefauver committee Senate hearings on organized crime in 1951 and the election night returns of the presidential race between Dwight Eisenhower and Adlai Stevenson in 1952. I remember, as a nine-year-old, being struck by the drama of the Kefauver hearings, the good guys (the senators) against the bad (the underworld), and it was *real*. I was riveted. I was also thrilled watching the broadcast of those 1952 election night returns. I remember sitting beside Baba, both of us rooting for General Eisenhower, who had saved the world from Nazism, and I couldn't understand why my mom and dad were supporting Stevenson.

The community I grew up in, Stamford, Connecticut, of the 1940s and 1950s, was like so many northeastern cities of that time, a melting pot of ethnic groups—Irish, Italian, German, Polish, Jewish and African-American. The suburbs hadn't yet developed to the point where they would draw a significant number of people (and resources) out of such cities. Most of us went to the same high school, the only public high school in Stamford. My family's first house, which sat a block from the railroad tracks in what would generously be called a lower-middle-class neighborhood, was flanked by a six-family walk-up on one side (the father of one of those families, I later learned, was a bookie) and a junkyard on the other. I'm sure there was racism and anti-Semitism in Stamford, as well as cronyism and crookedness among some of the businessmen and politicians, but personally I never saw or experienced any of this. Maybe I was blissfully unaware, or maybe such problems were overshadowed by the fact that we actually lived, worked and played together, that we were real people to one another. We were not concepts, not stereotypes. We were certainly not perfect. But we were neighbors and schoolmates.

My mother would have been the senator in our family if she had been born in my generation. Like my father, she always found time for charitable work. Mom is one of the most naturally outgoing, personable and caring people I've ever known, and has taught me so much about understanding and enjoying people. If you're going to live a public life, I don't think there's any question that you had better be someone who enjoys people. I went out to lunch in New Haven a couple of years ago with a friend. People kept coming up to our table, to say hello, to share their opinion on something, to ask how I felt about this or that. After a while my friend said, "God, this is rough. You don't have any privacy. People don't leave you *alone*." I responded, "You know, one thing worse than all these people coming over like this would be if no one came over."

Of course, there are times when people are annoying. And sometimes, like anyone else, I just want to be alone. But the fact is that, by definition, if you're going to be a public servant, most of your life is going to be *public*. You are expected to share it. When you go out, you will be noticed. You will be approached. If you can't handle that, let alone enjoy it, if you're not genuinely fed by and fascinated with human interaction, if you don't fundamentally *like* people, then this is probably not the career for you. There are very few loners or misanthropes on Capitol Hill or in America's statehouses or city halls.

When I was a kid, it was probably this enjoyment of people, as well as a still only vaguely understood desire to excel, that helped get me involved in my first "political" experiences in student government. I ran for president of my ninth-grade class in 1956 with a campaign speech featuring the titles of some of that era's hit rock-and-roll songs— "Earth Angel," "See You Later, Alligator," "Rock Around the Clock." After I won, one of my friends told me his social studies teacher said to his class, "I hope you didn't vote for Joe Lieberman just because he used those rock-and-roll songs in his speech."

The teacher's criticism of my "campaign" was on target. My platform was not built around too many issues. How many ninth-grade campaigns are? I wasn't dreaming of the U.S. Senate. I still imagined myself playing center field in the major leagues. But by the time I graduated from high school in the spring of 1960, I was definitely looking at public life as a possible career in an earnest way. The reason had everything to do with role models.

I don't think too many eighteen-year-olds today look at their political leaders the way I and much of my generation saw them in 1960. The succession of dignified, personable mayors who ran Stamford, the statewide leaders like Abe Ribicoff, Prescott Bush and Tom Dodd, the national leaders like Dwight Eisenhower and Adlai Stevenson—these men were, quite simply, figures of respect. That phrase sounds outdated and naive today, which is a shame. From the cop on the beat, whom we considered both a person of authority and our friend, to John F. Kennedy, who was about to become our next president and who symbolized the limitless possibility of our own lives, the world of my adolescence was filled with models to emulate.

Yes, there was much we did not know about some of these people, much we have come to learn. I'll talk a bit later about this kind of knowledge, about what I think we do and do not have a right to know about the private lives of public figures. But I can say here that our society needs, and will always benefit from, the sense of purpose and hope that I and most of my generation felt at the dawn of the 1960s.

Put this all together—my inherited appreciation for what America had provided my family, the ideal of service that was fundamental to my religious faith, the sense of community and connection I felt in the time and the place where I grew up, my belief in and the respect I had for figures of authority, the desire to make my own mark, and the hope and promise of a boundless future that seemed to lie ahead for our nation at the time I finished high school—and it explains why I had become focused on pursuing a public life by the time I began college at Yale in the fall of 1960.

It is impossible to overstate the impact of John Kennedy's election and 1961 inaugural address on our generation's sense of civic duty and public service. We've heard the words so often over the years—"Ask not what your country can do for you; ask what you can do for your country"—that it's easy to become numb to their meaning. Perhaps they no longer resonate the way they did when Kennedy spoke them that wintry January afternoon. But time cannot diminish their meaning and significance. In fact, it has increased them. If we are serious about righting what is wrong with politics and politicians in America today, we could do worse than repeat Kennedy's phrase to ourselves and act on it. Voting, of course, is the very least people can do. Opportunities for community and volunteer service in its myriad forms are there as well. And then there is public service itself, at every level, from local school or park boards, to political committees, to town councils, to regional, state and nationally elected positions.

We are privileged in this country—most of us—to be able to wake up each morning and not worry about survival. We have the luxury of being able to consider the purpose of our lives, to ask ourselves, in secular or spiritual terms, how we might make a difference during this time we are given on earth. We are also a very busy people and work very hard, sometimes at two jobs, often with both husband and wife at work. Yet millions of Americans find the time to volunteer in neighborhood, religious, athletic, social or community service groups, and still more millions could. There is also an abundance of nongovernmental helping professions in our society, from teaching to social work to work in community organizations, where you can make a living while making a difference. That, of course, is the satisfaction of these jobs, which, as the generation coming of age right now seems to realize, can be a reward far more enriching than money or material possessions.

The same reward awaits in government as well, in public life, as volunteer or professional, elected or civil servant. But it is important to acknowledge that government will not function with volunteers alone. It needs professionals—

hopefully some of the best and the brightest, willing and able to serve full-time in positions of public trust to make the government work. That is the spirit Kennedy's inaugural address stirred in me and so many of my generation.

One other personal motivation I haven't mentioned, which crystallized once I reached college, was the desire to make my family proud and certainly never to shame them. This is nothing unusual for any son or daughter. But I know that for me, simply having the opportunity to be the first in my family to attend college, knowing how hard my father worked his entire life to give me and my sisters this great opportunity which he never had, appreciating how intent he was on paying our way through school himself without seeking aid of any sort, realizing that this was his legacy to each of us—there was no way in the world I was going to let him down if I could help it. I had to succeed.

Which wasn't always easy. I arrived at Yale as an outsider, a public school kid among the preppies from Andover and Exeter. I had a rocky time with my classes the first semester, terrifying enough that I imagined I might be told to leave (I didn't realize then that Yale doesn't expel anyone who keeps trying). I kept trying, and by my second year my grades were good enough that I was able to lift my head from my books and begin getting involved in campus life. Both Whitney Griswold, the school's president at that time, and Kingman Brewster, who succeeded him during my junior year, impressed on us time and again that we were "chosen" to be at Yale, to receive this extraordinary education, and that with that privilege came an obligation to give back by striving for positions of leadership and service in society. To my ears, this was a very comfortable extension of the message I'd been hearing all my life, from the ethos of the covenant and *tikkun olam* to the challenge of JFK's inaugural address.

In lieu of a formal student government, which did not exist at Yale, the political heart of the campus was the university's newspaper, the *Yale Daily News*. It had a strong tradition of turning out politicians and journalists, notably political journalists. Bill Buckley was chairman of the *Daily News* during his time at Yale in the early 1950s and maintained a warm fraternal interest in each succeeding *News* board, including mine, regardless of its ideology. At the *News*, I worked with an extraordinarily talented group that has gone on to leadership in our country. David Gergen, who has served as adviser to Presidents Nixon, Reagan and Clinton, was the managing editor in the class before mine, and two of my classmates on the *News*, Bob Kaiser and Paul Steiger, became managing editors of the *Washington Post* and the *Wall Street Journal*, respectively.

As chairman of the *News*, which I became in 1962, the heart of my job was to write editorials, which forced me to form and express opinions on a wide range of public issues for the first time. The civil rights movement, with all that was happening in the South, became a focus for many of my columns. But I also wrote extensively about America's foreign policy, usually in support of Kennedy's muscular internationalism.

During the summer of 1963, I sought and received a student internship in Washington in the office of Connecticut's newly elected senator, Abe Ribicoff. To be in the capital city during the Kennedy administration, walking the streets and corridors of power, attending hearings and seeing the nation's leaders, was a thrill. But the opportunity to work for Ribicoff, to listen to him, watch him and learn from him, was truly a formative experience. Abe Ribicoff had been a very popular governor of Connecticut before coming to Washington in 1960, for two unsatisfying years as Kennedy's sec-

retary of Health, Education and Welfare. He returned home
in 1962 to run for the Senate and I worked part-time on his
winning campaign. Ribicoff was dignified in bearing, independent in politics and moderate in ideology. He was also
very good at building political relationships within his party
and outside of it that enabled him to get things done. And he
taught me about what he called "the integrity of compromise"—that it is usually better to compromise to make progress than to remain inflexible and therefore unproductive.
But I also saw that Ribicoff could be independent and pio-
neering, as when he was motivated by Rachel Carson's book
Silent Spring to do a series of hearings and pass legislation
regulating the use of pesticides. That was the first appearance on Capitol Hill of the new environmental movement.

Because I was in Washington during that summer of
1963, I also had another formative experience—the opportunity to participate in Dr. Martin Luther King's March on
Washington, which culminated at the Lincoln Memorial in
his soaring "I Have a Dream" speech. For me, this was
America at its best, America as my upbringing with family
and friends in Stamford had encouraged me to believe it
could be. Hundreds of thousands of us, of all religions, races
and nationalities, joined together peacefully but powerfully
to petition our government to right the wrong of racial bigotry. And the government, in the person of President
Kennedy himself, met the leaders of the march and promised
to act, as so many others of us there made similar, private
promises to ourselves to fight to end the injustice.

Soon after I returned to Yale that fall, the campus and
the city erupted in controversy after a student group invited
Governor George Wallace to speak in New Haven. My editorials defended the students' right to invite him and
Wallace's right to speak, no matter how we felt about his be-

liefs. Later that fall, inspired by Yale's chaplain, William Sloane Coffin, I led a group of classmates down to Mississippi to help register black voters for a "mock" election in that state, a prelude to the Mississippi Summer campaign of the following year. Along with hundreds of student volunteers from across the country, we slept in rows of sleeping bags on the floors of local homes and spent our days surrounded by conditions of segregation and poverty that most of us had only read about. I felt a definite sense of danger during the entire time I was there, the same danger that would result the following summer in the murders of James Chaney, Mickey Schwerner and Andy Goodman—three young men about the same age as I.

I spent the rest of my senior year, a year that included the heartbreaking assassination of President Kennedy, writing a thesis about John Bailey, who at that time headed both the Connecticut Democratic Party and the Democratic National Committee. I had heard Bailey's name for years. He looked like the classic old-school political "boss"—baggy pants, a cigar, eyeglasses propped up on his forehead. But he was more complicated than he appeared: wealthy from birth, well educated, tolerant and always open to change. He was the consummate political dealmaker, connected to just about every Democratic politician of any significance in the entire country, and most certainly in the state of Connecticut. Bailey was close to the Kennedys, and he was a major force in the rise of Abe Ribicoff. I had decided that state politics would probably be my profession, and I could see that there was no better way to learn about the history and intricacies of Connecticut's government than to study John Bailey. The hours I spent interviewing him that winter were priceless, my own private course in political science. And I spent other days talking with state government and political officials who not only gave me information and insights for my paper but also got to know me, which I understood might help if or when I entered politics myself. Like any profession, getting in the door can be the hardest part. That's one of the primary values of an internship in any field—getting to know some of the people who are already in the profession you'd like to enter, let alone acquiring the specialized knowledge that defines that profession.

I learned many practical political lessons from John Bailey. As I watched him organizing state political campaigns, overseeing and subtly influencing the nomination of Democratic candidates, and then coordinating and managing his party's program in the Connecticut legislature, I thought of the sentence from my then favorite novel, Robert Penn Warren's *All the King's Men*, in which the governor, Willie Stark, says to the reporter Jack Burden, "One thing I understand and you don't is what makes the mare go. I can make the mare go." John Bailey knew how to make the mare—government—go. He was a very partisan Democrat, but he knew how to bargain and engage in old-fashioned log-rolling to get things done so he could build a record for his Democratic governor or legislature, or deliver to an important constituency. The kind of political give-and-take Bailey was always involved in, with Democrats and Republicans, is sometimes seen as unseemly today, but it produced a lot more than today's rigid partisanship. Because Bailey brought to power an extraordinary group of Democratic governors—Chester Bowles, Abe Ribicoff, John Dempsey and Ella Grasso—and then helped them pass their programs through the legislature, his career greatly improved the lives of people in Connecticut.

John Bailey also taught me that politics can be very exciting—particularly campaigns in which the competition tests your skill and stamina. He also had a good time at what he did, showing me how working with a mix of diverse and colorful people campaigning and governing could be an awful lot of fun.

I spent the summer of 1964 with Chairman Bailey in Washington, because he had invited me to come down and work with him at the Democratic National Committee as they prepared for that fall's presidential election. I went to Atlantic City for the national convention, watched Lyndon Johnson receive the party's nomination and Bobby Kennedy electrify the convention, and then returned to New Haven to begin law school.

I went to law school because I thought it would help me be a better public official and would also provide an independent livelihood if my political career did not succeed, or until it did. At Yale Law School, I came to understand the law as the expression of our values, a reflection not just of what we consider right and wrong, but of our aspirations for ourselves. We don't always live up to the law, but it provides a standard for behavior. It represents the ideals and goals we have for ourselves as a society, like the values and commandments of religion. An image I once read of the law that I love is that in hell there is nothing but laws because people there do only evil if left on their own; in heaven there is *no* law because it's simply not needed; and here on earth we're somewhere in between, with law helping guide us in our aspirations toward heaven.

When I graduated from law school, I was eager to begin pursuing such heavenly aspirations along the very earthly path of practical politics in Connecticut. Before I move on to that chapter, I would like to add a few thoughts for those, like my student interns, who may be thinking about a career in politics. The upbringing, early experiences and historical context I have described here are mine. They are personal. If you are thinking about entering public life, the course that you follow will be your own. Not every future elected official needs to go to law school or write a college paper on a local party chairman as I did. What I think is most important is that you first read and study history and political philosophy, as I also did, to understand what has preceded you, to find your heroes and mentors in the past if not the present, to shape your own ideals and to begin to decide whether you are interested in participating. Then you should find opportunities for practical experiences in government and politics so that you can determine whether the reality of public life is as satisfying to you as the thought of it. Hopefully, this book will begin to give you a feel for that reality. Then, of course, I hope you decide to enter the arena, as I did when I left law school and settled in New Haven in 1967.

3

MOUNTING
A FIRST CAMPAIGN

LAST SUMMER, early in his campaign for this year's Democratic Party presidential nomination, Bill Bradley wondered aloud to a reporter about the enmity that seems to inevitably arise between candidates in a political race. "The question is," asked Bradley, "can you have a politics that becomes a little bit like the McGwire-Sosa home-run contest last year? One of them won the title, but both of them won in terms of what the competition produced for the baseball fans. Why can't politics be like that?"

Well, sometimes it can and is, but more often it is not, because unlike the home-run contest, where both Mark Mc-Gwire and Sammy Sosa were heralded as winners and heroes, in a political campaign there is only one winner. Even where both candidates are honorable, thoughtful and not nasty by nature, there is a lot on the line, and eventually there are going to be people on both sides who will push their candidate to distinguish himself or herself from the other candidate, to give people a clear reason to vote for him or her and not the other. This is when a campaign runs the risk of slipping from appropriate discussion, debate and even attack centered around facts, values and ideas to inappropriate misstatements, personal assaults and innuendoes based on distortions and fictions.

Unfortunately the latter has become the norm in American political campaigning at all levels of government. And the American public—those not enlisted in the partisan armies that divide current political battlefields—has made it clear that they're sick and tired of it. To describe the effect of all this negative campaigning, I make the analogy of Kmart launching an all-out advertising offensive against Wal-Mart, and Wal-Mart doing the same in return. The net effect would be that fewer people would shop at either place. They might decide not to shop at all, or they might just go over to JCPenney. This is where Ross Perot and, most recently, Jesse Ventura have found much of their support—as an alternative to "politics as usual," which unfortunately, in the campaign phase, is too often negative politics.

Again, there is nothing new about this. For most of our history, candidates have naturally tried to distinguish themselves from their opponents, usually by criticizing them. And third parties have regularly appeared, but usually as part of a political realignment around a major societal change. But what is happening today seems different, in part because negative campaigning has the added reach and sharp edge of modern television marketing, but also because the third-party response seems less like Lincoln's Republican Party and Teddy Roosevelt's Bull Moose Party and more a reflection of Henry David Thoreau's hostility to the entire process of popular elections, which he described as "a sort of gaming, like chequers or backgammon."* Third parties today seem to

---

* *Quoted in Garry Wills*, A Necessary Evil *(New York: Simon & Schuster, 1999), p. 264.*

be reactions against the politics of the two major parties rather than coalitions formed to advance an idea or cause.

That brings me back to the question Bill Bradley was asking, and it is a perennial one: whether it is possible for political candidates to stay completely focused on ideas and solutions, to run a "positive" campaign and to compete without the element of attack, all of which would probably make today's third parties less attractive. It is possible, but it isn't easy. I'm afraid, based on my own experience, that you cannot pretend your opponent, along with his platform of policies, does not exist—unless, of course, you are confident you are so far ahead of him that you can ignore him, and that can be risky, as my opponent, the incumbent U.S. senator, found out in 1988. In most campaigns, you are going to have to compare his or her platform to yours. You are going to have to compare him or her to you. If you are a challenger, you are, as a political consultant once succinctly told me, going to have to convince the voters to "fire him and hire you."

I had my first personal experience with the reality of political campaigning in 1970, when I mounted a campaign for a seat in the Connecticut state senate.

I was three years out of law school. I had taken a job with the New Haven law firm Wiggin and Dana, become active in the local political and Jewish communities, chaired a statewide Citizens for Kennedy group (which at the age of twenty-six drew some attention) during Bobby Kennedy's tragically brief presidential campaign in 1968, become part of a statewide Democratic coalition built on the remnants of Kennedy's and Eugene McCarthy's supporters after Nixon was elected president that fall, done some lobbying in the Connecticut legislature for several of our law firm's clients, including the state hospital association, and kept my eyes

open for the best opportunity to make my own entry into political office.

That opportunity emerged in the form of a state senate
seat in New Haven then held by Ed Marcus, the Democratic
majority leader of the state senate, a powerful, smart and
feared politician. When he announced in late 1969 that he
was going to make a run for the U.S. Senate the next year, he
made it clear that if he didn't get that nomination he was
going to come back for his state legislative seat. There were
plenty of people in line to replace Marcus in the state senate,
but none of them tried. Either they did not want to incur his
wrath or they did not think he was beatable.

A challenger rarely defeats an incumbent solely on the
challenger's own merits. The incumbent has to have vulnerabilities. Unless there is some overriding context or influence
that sweeps an incumbent out of office on a wave not of his
making (such as the Republican "revolution" of 1994), he really ought to get reelected, if he is doing his job, and if he has
not made too many enemies in the process.

Ed Marcus had rankled feelings in the state Democratic
Party hierarchy, squaring off over the years against the governor and other party leaders. Political independence is
generally an asset as far as I'm concerned, but Marcus's independence bruised some people. The result was that by 1970
the most powerful Connecticut Democrats, including Senator Abe Ribicoff, Governor John Dempsey and party chairman John Bailey, were estranged from Ed Marcus. More
locally, I sensed that as Marcus's statewide power and responsibility had grown, a gap had developed between him and a
lot of the people in his state senate district. In fact, the demo-
graphics of the district were changing under him. While I
was in Hartford lobbying for my law firm, I had also become
excited about the prospects for making a difference in the

state legislature. The late 1960s was a time when state governments in America were becoming more significant and more professional, with new state initiatives in areas of public concern like urban redevelopment, civil rights and environmental protection.

Besides, unlike the politicians who were ahead of me in line to replace Marcus but were afraid to lose the positions they had, I had nothing to protect. I was only twenty-seven, with a career that was just beginning. Maybe because I was twenty-seven I never thought much about what would have happened to that career if Marcus had won and been in a position to get even. But I can say that throughout my public life—in that 1970 race, in 1982 when I ran for state attorney general and in my 1988 U.S. Senate campaign—the biggest strides forward have come when I've taken the biggest risks. I was a complete long shot against Ed Marcus, but I thought I could do a better job for the district and I wanted to get my political career moving, so I decided to run.

It was the first time I had to choose a theme for a campaign, the reason people should vote for me. Our choice, unaided by polls or consultants, was that I would be a "Strong New Voice for a Better New Haven," which sounds to me today a lot like the simple, traditional call "It's time for a change."

Because of political and community work I'd done over the preceding few years in New Haven, I had a local base of support—in the Jewish community, in the black community and at Yale—that helped me start organizing. We began raising money, but fund-raising in 1970 was not what it is today, especially for a state senate campaign. Television, which dominates virtually every aspect of campaigning today at almost all levels of politics and which is exorbitantly costly, was not a factor for us. Any television exposure we got came from occasional news coverage, not from advertising. We spent a little bit on radio ads toward the end of the campaign, but most of our advertising that year was done in newspapers and on billboards, which today seem to have gone out of fashion. Professional media consultants now will tell you that "static" ads—in newspapers, on billboards, on the sides of buses (which are not totally static)—don't do much more than tell people your name. If you're unknown, they say, such ads can be useful in terms of raising your recognition and introducing you to the public, but other than that, advertising money is much better spent on the electronic media—television, radio and, most recently, the newly emerging political medium of the Internet—which communicate a message.

Our total budget for that 1970 campaign was $30,000, the most ever raised at that time by a state senate challenger, but a long way from the $190,000 that one Connecticut state senator spent to get elected in 1998 or the $4.9 million I raised for my 1994 U.S. Senate campaign, which is nothing compared to the $39.9 million Michael Huffington spent during his 1994 campaign for a Senate seat in California, or the $57.7 million George W. Bush raised in just nine months last year. These are astounding numbers, almost incomprehensible. It's one measure of how drastically politics has changed in the last thirty years.

Most of our money in that 1970 race was spent on what is typically called retail politics—literally going door-to-door to connect with the voters. Some presidential candidates still do this for the caucuses and primaries in places like Iowa and New Hampshire. The number of people who turn out in those elections is so relatively small that going door-to-door can actually make a difference, both with the people you meet face-to-face and with the people *they* talk to after meeting you, as it did for me in 1970.

The New Haven state senate district that year had about 30,000 voters, and roughly 7,000 of those people would cast ballots in the Democratic primary election, which, in an area as overwhelmingly Democratic as New Haven at that time, was tantamount to the general election itself.

I personally visited more than 3,000 homes or apartments in my 1970 state senate campaign. We had an army of young, energetic campaign volunteers—a children's crusade, really—who fanned out into the community day after day for me or with me. Among them was a very personable and memorable Yale Law student from Arkansas named Bill Clinton. We didn't have the machinery, the veteran political organization, that Ed Marcus had, but I did have the personal endorsement of New Haven's popular former mayor Dick Lee, who had adopted me in a way, and of Abe Ribicoff, who had developed into my mentor by then. Both of them had had conflicts with Marcus. If I had been running against almost anyone else, Ribicoff probably would not have gotten involved because U.S. senators normally stay out of state or local intraparty struggles. Although I am a real skeptic about the impact on voters of one politician endorsing another, when Ribicoff and Lee stepped into this one, it drew a lot of attention and gave me the credibility I didn't have on my own. People began to believe that this might actually become a contest.

That campaign developed into a tough struggle, which brings me back to the subject of attack politics and negative campaigning. I challenged Ed Marcus on a number of issues, votes and acts in his career. He came back at me in the same direct way. It was a rough fight, but it was fair in the sense that it was based on facts, and that's the crucial difference, I believe, between appropriately making the case for your election and inappropriately indulging in negative, attack campaigning. If the content of your attack is factual, relevant and fair, then you've done your job and it's up to the voters to decide. If, on the other hand, your facts aren't right, or they are manipulated to the point of untruth, if your approach is to pull down your opponent in any way possible, even if it requires going into his purely personal life, then you've gone over the line into negative, attack campaigning.

On the night of the primary election, with all but one ward reporting, I was behind Marcus by ten votes. The remaining ward was inhabited mostly by Yale students and African-Americans and was coordinated for me by my friend Lanny Davis, then a law student, now a prominent Washington lawyer. Lanny called us excitedly at headquarters to say he thought we had won the ward handily but one of the opposition ward workers had intentionally jammed the voting machines. We immediately dispatched a phalanx of young lawyers and called for help from election officials. They opened the machines and I carried that ward by 250 votes, giving me a victory by 240 or roughly 4 percent of the total votes cast.

One of the many lessons John Bailey taught me was: "In politics, you should always work to convince your opponents in the last election to become your supporters in the next election." That took a while for Ed Marcus and me, but eventually the bad memories faded. In 1988, he actively supported me for the U.S. Senate, and later became Democratic state chairman of Connecticut, where he and I have worked very well together.

In 1970, I had seen an opportunity and taken it. That state senate district was ready for a change. The campaign was enormously exciting but it wasn't easy or without risk. I had challenged a very strong and able incumbent and won, because I was able to present myself as a candidate of change with new ideas and because I received wonderful support from a large corps of volunteers, most of them young. We had a few big-name endorsements, but my campaign organization was otherwise an army of amateurs. For me, American democracy had lived up to its promise of openness in Connecticut's tenth state senatorial district. The local machine had been defeated. I hope the story of this first campaign of my career encourages you, the reader, to see how outsiders can become insiders in our political system with a lot of hard work and a little luck. It certainly encouraged me to be optimistic as I prepared to go to Hartford full of ideas about how to use my newly won office to get some things done for my city and state.

4

STRAIGHT
AND HONEST

My starting salary as a state senator in 1971 was $4,000 a year. No one wants to hear a politician talk about being underpaid, but salaries for state government officials across the nation at the time I began my career were notoriously low. This has changed in many places since then (although not everywhere, and not enough), but if you were a state senator in Connecticut in 1971 and you weren't already wealthy, that meant you almost certainly had another job as well.

I had two. At the time I ran for the senate I was working as counsel for the New Haven Equal Opportunities Commission and as an assistant dean at Yale. Two years later I left the Yale position and joined another lawyer in forming a private law partnership in New Haven. Although the job of state senator was supposed to be part-time—in the idealized spirit of limited government and citizen legislators—it was, in fact, at least full-time. That meant I had two full-time jobs during my ten years in the state senate, and the pressure was enormous. I felt at times as if I were riding three horses at once. I was married by then, with two young children, and like so many people that age, getting started with both a family and a career, I was hustling. If there was ever a time in my public life when I might have been vulnerable to direct, unethical pressures and influences involving money, it would have been then.

An incident early in my career as a state senator still sticks in my mind. The executives of a company approached me in my capacity as an attorney and asked me to represent them in a real estate transaction. This company was at the same time involved in obtaining environmental permits in another matter from the state. There would have been nothing illegal about doing the real estate work, but there was the clear possibility of the appearance of a conflict of interest, and I felt uncomfortable. So I asked a veteran colleague of mine in the state legislature, an attorney himself and a savvy guy, about it.

"How do you make a judgment," I asked him, "about whether to take this kind of case?"

He answered without hesitation.

"It depends," he said, "on the size of the fee."

Those cynical words went right through my gut. I turned down the client, but that conversation taught me a lesson and reminded me of a book I had read in college in which a caricatured Tammany Hall boss had distinguished between "honest graft" and "dishonest graft." The latter included bribery, which is unusual in politics today, although it sometimes happens, even in Washington, as the Abscam scandal showed us not so long ago.

"Honest graft," which the old Tammany boss described as "seein' your opportunities and takin' 'em," is a different matter. The "size of the fee" rule for deciding whether to take that client sounded a lot like "honest graft." I remember when cable television franchises were first given out by the state government in the 1960s. Every one of the franchised boards in the various regions of Connecticut had local and state politicians on them, and many of those politicians earned a good deal of money when the franchises were fully developed years later. Was this illegal? No. It was "honest graft." Was it fair and likely to encourage trust in government? I don't think so.

In post-Watergate America, that kind of behavior is rare. But more subtle opportunities and temptations remain, particularly for officials at the state and local levels who are either poorly paid or work part-time. I remember how liberated I felt in 1982 when I was elected Connecticut's attorney general and was paid a salary ($50,000) that allowed me to work full-time for the public.

People in public office, especially at local and state levels of government, are squeezed by many of the same financial and family pressures that so many others are. But unlike most people, politicians have power, which can be worth something, and therefore they are faced with opportunities and ethical challenges others are not.

That doesn't excuse questionable behavior or unethical decisions. It certainly doesn't excuse illegal actions. Although public figures may face the same everyday pressures as the people we represent, we are not, and should not be, judged by the same standards. More should be expected of us, by the nature of the offices we hold and the responsibilities that come with them. We are public officials, not private citizens. Everything we do can become public and therefore has serious consequences for the community. We are—whether we like it or not—role models. We have voluntarily entered a contract with the voters that is based on trust. If we violate that trust, our government, our democracy, suffers. So the first question a public figure must always ask himself when making a decision about his personal behavior or actions, about whether to take an opportunity, is not just "Is it legal?" but "Is it *right?*"

When public figures begin to separate these two questions, the foundation of trust between the people and their leaders is compromised. During the past several years, the American people have watched too many public figures in both parties try to make distinctions between whether something is legal and whether it is right. The consequences for our politics have been disastrous because the people correctly see these as attempts to rationalize behavior that is wrong, and they turn away disgusted.

I assume that everything I do in my life—*everything*—could possibly become public and therefore I should not do anything privately that I could not justify publicly. This working principle probably resulted in part from some of the formative national experiences of my early political life such as Vietnam and Watergate, where behavior that was initially private led to rebuke and dishonor for Presidents Lyndon Johnson and Richard Nixon when it became public. It also came, I am sure, from more local experiences like my own bitter entry into politics in 1970, and the ensuing two years in which everything I did was subject to public questioning by my opponent and his allies; I learned early to be careful. More personally, I was raised with twin fears of bringing shame on my family and failing to uphold the principles of my faith. The words of the Twenty-seventh Psalm, "Lead me on the path of integrity because of them that lie in wait for me," have special meaning for contemporary politicians, which is not surprising since the psalmist himself was a superb politician.

During my state government service I asked my staff to imagine how they would feel if they knew that a particular action or decision we were about to make would be questioned the following morning in banner headlines on the front pages of our state's newspapers. The question should

not be whether it was legal (hopefully we would not know-
ingly do anything illegal) but whether we could answer to the
satisfaction of the public why we had taken that action and if
we could live with that answer politically and personally. We
called that our "Front Page Rule" and still try to live by it.

These are not always easy decisions. Throughout my
public life I have struggled with them and watched political
colleagues do the same. Most of us realize that the contemporary media are so intrusive and our responsibilities as role
models are so great that we must embody, in our public and
private lives, the best values of the people we represent.
When we do not, there is erosion of our moral authority and
the public's trust in us, which are critical to our ability to
lead, to persuade, to mobilize public opinion and to build a
consensus behind a common agenda. President Clinton and
all of us in public life today have learned that lesson painfully
from the Lewinsky scandal. We must remember it well in the
years ahead, or we and our political system will pay an even
greater price.

One of my heroes, Teddy Roosevelt, put it plainly: "My
power vanishes into thin air the instant my fellow citizens,
who are straight and honest, cease to believe that I represent
them and fight for what is straight and honest. That is all the
strength I have."

When an elected official's conduct does fall short and he
is tempted to slide into legalizations, rationalizations or half-
truths to explain or excuse it, he is merely compounding the
problem. The public wants instead a quick and honest ad-
mission of error, an apology and perhaps a plea for forgive-
ness. If they are given that, they will usually respond with
remarkable fairness and tolerance. This is what the American
people want most of all from their leaders, particularly at this
time: to follow Teddy Roosevelt's simple counsel in word and

deed—to behave "straight and honest," and when they don't, to admit it "straight and honest."

That should not discourage anyone from considering a career in public life, because it is no more than most people expect from their family, friends and co-workers. And it is no less than those who are chosen to lead owe their constituents.

5

LOSING

ALTHOUGH MY LIFE as a state senator was hassled, my work was very fulfilling. For the first time I experienced the thrill of transforming a proposal into a law, and learned how to make that happen. Through personal trial and error and by watching more-experienced legislators, I learned how to relate to constituents, colleagues, interest groups and the media.

In 1970, Connecticut voters elected a Republican governor, Tom Meskill, and gave Democrats a slim 19–17 margin in the state senate, so I learned quickly about the necessity of bipartisan cooperation to make government work. Because of the large number of committees in the Connecticut general assembly, I was able to become chairman of a senate committee—the State and Urban Development Committee—during my first term. Connecticut's legislative committees were bicameral and joint, and functioned almost always by consensus, which gave me another unusual opportunity to expand my education in legislative cooperation. I worked successfully with my committee colleagues to propose more effective ways for the state to assist the central cities, including my own city of New Haven, and to develop new methods for using the state's tax-exempt bor-

rowing power to provide financing for commercial, industrial and residential development through the Connecticut
Development Authority and the Connecticut Housing Finance Authority. When the media raised questions about the
skyrocketing costs of the construction of a new University of
Connecticut Health Center, my committee launched an investigation that led to an unprecedented series of public
hearings documenting infuriating governmental inefficien-
cies and disheartening corruption. We recommended reforms in public works procedures that were adopted. Because
my staff resources were extremely limited, I asked Bill
Bonvillian, a student intern from Yale Divinity School, to be
the staff director of the health center investigation and report. He did a great job, and seventeen years later rejoined
me as legislative director of my U.S. Senate office.

During my early years in the Connecticut state senate, I
became very active in two other policy areas: environmental
protection and criminal justice. Those were the post–Earth
Day years, when the modern environmental movement was
born. In Connecticut, we created the State Department of
Environmental Protection and adopted laws to clean our air
and water. For me, it was the beginning of a career-long devotion to environmental protection and natural resource
conservation, and provided me with a powerful example of
how the law can change behavior. Without those environmental protection laws, and ones like them throughout the
country, our air and water would be far more dirty and unhealthy than they are today, more of our open spaces would
be developed and the societal consensus embracing environmental protection never would have formed.

In the area of criminal justice, I experienced a different
kind of change. The liberal, criminal rights–oriented theo-
ries I took with me from law school ran smack into the real-

ity of violent crime and street crime in my New Haven neighborhood. I knew people who were victims of violent crime and muggings; my house was broken into twice. Fear of crime was constricting freedom and stifling growth in our once proud and thriving city. So I began to propose tougher criminal laws, including the death penalty, and to focus more on victims' rights and expedited criminal procedures.

As I look back, I realize I was developing an independent, nonideological agenda that was, however, not antigovernmental. That led me naturally in 1974 to become an early and very involved supporter of the gubernatorial campaign of Congresswoman Ella Grasso. I was one of Ella's top policy advisers and traveled around the state with and for her. She won a landslide victory that helped Democrats carry twenty-nine of the thirty-six state senate districts. I was elected senate majority leader. Most of the twenty-nine Democrats were new to the state senate, which meant that they were not hesitant to choose a relative newcomer like me as their leader.

Ella Grasso was the first woman in American history to be elected governor of a state in her own right—that is, without succeeding her husband. She was a New Democrat before anyone coined the term, working to balance the state budget; to attract businesses which would create jobs; to promote better ways to help those who could not help themselves; and to reflect mainstream values of opportunity, hard work, responsibility and integrity in her leadership. I learned a lot about governance and public policy in my years as Governor Ella Grasso's state senate majority leader.

We inherited a budget deficit and began our time of leadership with a series of crises and disputes, including several with traditional Democratic constituencies. For example, state employees and city officials had expected immediate, substantial increases in support, not spending restraints from a Democratic governor and legislature. There were no programmatic solutions to our problems that would please everyone and so, as a harbinger of the gridlock I would face years later in the U.S. Senate, we were unable to agree on a budget. As we approached the end of the fiscal year in 1975 and the prospect of government shutdowns, the governor and we in leadership finally agreed on a budget plan. We told her she had to come to a joint house and senate Democratic caucus that evening, to personally plead for support, after which we would ask our colleagues to stand with us behind her. She was masterful in her appeal, acknowledging the unpopularity of all the available options, bluntly reminding our colleagues that many of them would not be there if she had not been elected with such a huge margin, and arguing that we, as Democrats, had to prove we could make the tough decisions and govern responsibly. After the other leaders and I endorsed the program, she thanked us movingly and then received a standing vote of support and sustained applause. As the governor departed the room, the deputy speaker of the house, Bob Vicino of Bristol, turned to me and said, "This should prove to you, Joe, that a friend in need is a pain in the ass." He was right, of course, but that painful decision and others like it helped lead Connecticut to more effective state government and better economic times. Before long, the state employees and city leaders who had been so unhappy were given the support they needed.

Each legislative day, I would meet with my partner in the senate leadership, the president pro tem, Joe Fauliso of Hartford, a wise and experienced politician, and we would go over the senate calendar, deciding which items were ready for action. We would then take that list to the daily caucus of Democratic senators where all the bills were discussed. A great premium was put on achieving consensus, except in matters of personal conscience like abortion. In other words, we would usually not take up a bill on the floor unless all Democrats were prepared to support it. I would then meet with the senate Republican leader to negotiate the final list of bills, to hear what changes his members wanted and to see whether we could accommodate them. In the end, there was of course some partisan disagreement, particularly on signature proposals like the budget, but most of the work was done with bipartisan consent. And the disagreements were not divisive. We remained remarkably civil with one another. In fact, the two Republican leaders during my time as majority leader, Lew Rome and Dick Bozzuto, became my good personal friends.

As the years passed in the state senate, I began to think about what my next political opportunity might be. In politics, you start with a commitment to public service and then try to find a good place to carry out that commitment. But there are far too many variables for you to plot out a rigid career path. Naturally, you will have goals, but you also have to keep your options open about where you will be able to achieve those goals. I dreamed of being governor and, if I was lucky, ending up in the U.S. Senate someday. But I couldn't see my way clearly from the state senate to the next step on the way to those dreams. One office I never specifically considered was a seat the U.S. House of Representatives. But there are certain traditional rules in politics that most politicians follow, and one of them is to take an opportunity for service in a higher office when it comes, because it may never come again. Sometimes political opportunities arise in unforeseen places, at unexpected times. I've watched people refuse to seize the moment when such an opportunity presented itself, and they have regretted that decision the rest of their lives. Pursuing such an opportunity, however, does not guarantee success, as I learned in 1980.

During the early spring of that year Bob Giaimo, the congressman from my New Haven district, suddenly and surprisingly announced his retirement. After almost ten years in the state senate I was ready for a move. I consulted my closest allies in the state and local Democratic organizations, and I decided this was an opportunity I could not let pass by, even though I had never before considered it, so I entered the race.

It was the first campaign in which I hired professional pollsters and media consultants. In fact, my pollsters were Mark Penn and Doug Schoen, two young Harvard graduates who would go on in the 1990s to become very successful polltakers and advisers for President Clinton. No candidate should seek office without a clear purpose, a message, a reason for the voters to "hire" him. My consultants and I decided mine would be that I was a "proven leader" the people in my district could count on, based on my experience as state senate majority leader. As we entered the last month of the campaign, that approach seemed to be working. According to our internal polling, three weeks before the election I was ahead by nineteen points.

Unfortunately, that poll was our last. We had committed what remained of the $300,000 we had raised in that campaign to running TV and radio ads accentuating my experience. We had conducted a positive campaign, focusing on my strengths rather than my opponent's weaknesses. The only ripple of concern with that nineteen-point lead was that a third of the people questioned in the poll were undecided. I was uneasy about that, but my consultants said it was natural, since my opponent and I were not well-known incumbents.

Today I would have run daily tracking polls right up to the election, but at that time the strategy of polling, the technology of computers and, most importantly, my financial resources were less developed.

It turned out that my uneasiness was justified. First, my opponent, Larry DeNardis, a college professor and a moderate Republican, went on the offensive, launching a series of television ads over those last three weeks sharply attacking me as a high-taxing, big-spending liberal. He also began warm and wonderful radio ads highlighting his ethnic heritage, which, in a district as heavily populated with Italian-Americans as ours, might move some voters. I became anxious and asked the media consultants whether we should respond, counterattack, do something forceful in return. But they said to stay the course. We had built our nineteen-point lead by taking the high ground, and we should stay there.

That might have worked had it not been for a national tidal wave of frustration with the status quo and desire for change which we had not seen coming and which expressed itself in swelling support for Ronald Reagan's candidacy. My television and radio message of proven leadership and closeness to the Democratic establishment was jarringly out of sync with the public mood. I ran ahead of President Carter but not enough to avoid defeat.

Some lessons are learned only through experience, and here are a few that I learned from my loss in 1980:

> • A candidate must keep polling right up until the end, and be prepared to conduct the campaign accordingly. In 1980, I needed a more active message than "proven leadership." I should have emphasized some of the ways in which I would have fought for the district's voters in Washington.

- You cannot allow your opponent's attacks to go unanswered. In 1980, I should have gone on the air to show, from my record, that I was not a high-taxing big spender. And, maybe, I could have pointed to the vulnerabilities in my opponent's voting record.

- You will have a hard time winning a modern political campaign if you don't hire professional consultants, but you may well lose if you do everything they tell you to do—that is, if you don't consider as well what you have learned in your own political experience and from the voters themselves. In 1980, I listened to the consultants instead of acting on my political instincts.

- Finally, success in politics, as in life, depends not only on hard work but also on good luck. It helps to run in a good year, and 1980 was not a good year for a Democrat in my congressional district.

Losing a political election is a very painful, emotional experience, in part because it is so visible and in part because we politicians are so competitive. Like a professional athlete whose success or failure is witnessed by a crowd of spectators, a politician "performs," if you will, in public. Unlike an athlete, however, his success or failure is directly determined by the audience. They don't just boo or cheer. They vote you in or out. We candidates are, after all, seeking their approval. If it is denied, that is clear and it hurts. You can't help taking it personally.

In the wake of that 1980 loss, I felt wounded and embarrassed, for myself, for my family, for my friends. I'll never forget a photograph that ran in the next morning's New

Haven newspaper of my son, Matt, my daughter, Rebecca, and me. Matt, who was thirteen at the time, was next to me on the couch in our hotel suite headquarters as the late returns continued to come in. I had my hand on his forehead, pushing his hair back. He and Rebecca had the saddest looks on their faces, and I appeared simply stunned, which I was. My parents, who were there as well, startled me with their equanimity. I would have guessed that they would have broken down, each in their own way: my mother sad and sobbing, my father's face grim with remorse. But there was none of that. They seemed fine, which surprised and reassured me. It was not until a year ago that my mother told me how devastated they both had been that night. "We held ourselves together for you," she said. "Then we went home and just fell apart." It took them weeks, she told me, to get over it. And I never knew until years later.

I had to get over it, too, which was going to be difficult. More difficult, however, and more immediately pressing than any professional and political concerns, was the condition of my marriage.

Betty Haas and I had met in the summer of 1963, when we were both working as interns in Senator Ribicoff's office. Betty was a student at Smith College, interested in politics and public service just as I was. She was inspired, as I was, by the ideals of President Kennedy, and as we fell in love we were drawn also by the prospect of combining public service with marriage and a family. We married in 1965, had our first child, Matt, in 1967, and our second child, Rebecca, in 1969. When I ran for the state senate in 1970, Betty was my campaign treasurer. Our conversations at home at the end of the day would be whether certain checks had been deposited, whether this bill or that one had been paid, how we were going to pay for a particular radio or newspaper ad. That's how much our public and private lives were merged, and looking back, I can see it was too much.

Betty and I were young when we married, in our early twenties and still developing as individuals. We were still in our twenties, with an infant and a toddler, when I was first elected to the state senate. During the ten years I served in the state legislature, Betty and I began to take diverging paths in life, and our marriage became troubled. By the time I ran for Congress in 1980, we were attending couples counseling, trying in every way we could to resolve the problems in our relationship. When the election was over, we both turned fully to our marriage, free from the pressure of politics. But by the middle of the following year we agreed that it just wasn't going to work and we separated. Not long thereafter we were divorced. It was the most difficult and painful decision I had ever made.

There was no single reason our marriage failed. Some of it had to do with the different directions in which our personalities and careers developed. Some of it was related to the fact that I had become much more religiously observant than I was when we met and married. And there is no doubt that some of it was caused by the demands my political career put on our private life. That is surely one of the great costs and risks of public life.

My divorce left me with a second loss to deal with in 1981. No one in my family had ever divorced. It wasn't supposed to happen to good people, so divorce to me meant failure.

Full of guilt, I moved into an apartment in a two-family house in New Haven owned and occupied by my sister and brother-in-law. Betty continued her career as a psychiatric social worker and I returned to private law practice full time, but we both focused on the children. They were still our shared top priority. Because Betty and I continued to live in New Haven, we were able to work out a joint custody arrangement in which Matt and Rebecca spent half of the week with each of us. We began to rebuild and move forward with the children in as healthy a way as possible. As I look at these two young adults now, I believe we succeeded, or, to put it better, they succeeded. Matt went to law school and now teaches English in New Haven. Rebecca also went to law school and now works with a private social service agency in New York.

Interestingly, none of my political opponents has ever raised the issue of my divorce and tried to use that against me. The only time it surfaced in my entire career was after the speech I gave in September 1998 about President Clinton's relationship with Monica Lewinsky. There were letters to the editor in various newspapers asking what gave a divorced man the right to be so morally self-righteous. A popular radio talk show in New Haven received a call from a woman who claimed that my marriage broke up because I committed adultery, followed by a caller who said that was untrue because he knew my marriage had ended when my wife died. I was in Washington and heard about this radio program only later, but a friend of Betty's was listening and immediately called her. Betty was so upset that *she* called in and told the talk-show host and his listening audience two things in no uncertain terms. First, like Mark Twain, the rumors of her death were greatly exaggerated. And second, she said she knew I had never committed adultery.

This is just one unusual example of how the boundaries between one's public and private lives can become blurred in politics, and where the truth can be blurred as well, unless you are fortunate to have someone, including an ex-spouse, tell the truth.

One surprising, positive aspect of losing that 1980 election was that it helped me put my political career in perspective. For several weeks after the loss, people greeted me with great and sincere sympathy. At first I appreciated it, but then it made me uncomfortable and ultimately unhappy. I remember saying to myself, as the condolences continued, "I didn't die. I just lost an election. I'm only thirty-eight, and I've got a lot of things I can yet do with my life."

The most comforting and inspiring message I received after the 1980 election came from Father Joseph Dilion, whom I used to call "my parish priest" because his church, St. Brendan's, was in the New Haven neighborhood where I lived. Father Dilion telephoned me and said, "Don't let this stop you, Joe. God is saving you for something better."

I went back to law practice and thought about other ways to serve the community. While I considered seeking an appointive position in government, or working for a nonprofit organization, perhaps a university, I ultimately came back to elected office as the career choice that gave me the greatest opportunity for service, satisfaction and happiness.

There was a statewide election in 1982. Bill O'Neill, who had become governor when Ella Grasso died of cancer in 1980, was running for reelection, so there was no opening there. But the incumbent Democratic attorney general was thought to be considering retirement, so I began to focus on that office as my best opportunity to get back into public service. Compared to our neighboring states of New York and Massachusetts, Connecticut's attorney general was surprisingly passive and still served part-time. That would be my campaign message: The Attorney General's office has more unused potential for public good than any other in the state government. I promised to be the people's lawyer, full time, fighting particularly for them in consumer and environmental protection.

So, on a bleak, snowy afternoon in December 1981, standing on the plaza in front of the Connecticut Supreme Court Building in Hartford, with only a handful of family and friends, and two steadfast political allies, Vinny Mauro and Ben DiLieto, New Haven's Democratic town chairman and mayor, respectively, I declared my candidacy for the Democratic nomination for attorney general. Although I realized that while one defeat can be a character builder, losing two elections in a row would probably mean the end of my political career, I was more relaxed and optimistic than I had been in a long time. I think that was because of my genuine excitement about what I could do as attorney general, and because of the lessons I had learned in my 1980 loss. I remember what a friend in business told me at that time: "I'd much rather hire somebody who has been knocked on his rear end and shown he could get back up on his feet than somebody who has never had to deal with a loss."

As I worked for a political comeback, my personal life took a new turn as well, on Easter Sunday 1982. Through a mutual friend acting as a matchmaker, I was introduced to a woman in New York named Hadassah Freilich Tucker, who was also divorced and had a six-year-old son, Ethan. In what strikes me now as an embarrassing but hilarious example of the intersection of public and private lives, I called Hadassah on that Sunday and explained, "I'm running for attorney general, and because today is Easter Sunday, I have no political schedule. I'd love to meet you, but if I can't do it today, I won't be able to come to New York until after election day in November." Hadassah's response was appropriately direct and utilitarian. "Great," she said. "I just bought a new dining room table and chairs, and I need someone to help me move them in, so please come down." It was chemistry at first conversation and, later that day, love at first sight. And incidentally, I found it possible on a surprising number of occasions between Easter and election day to find my way to New York.

Hadassah wasn't particularly political, although she had worked in government relations and policy planning for a couple of corporations. Her parents, Samuel and Ella Freilich, were both survivors of the Holocaust who had met and married in Prague (where Hadassah was born) after the war and come to America in 1949 after the Communists seized power in Czechoslovakia. They settled in Gardner, Massachusetts, where Hadassah's father served as the community's rabbi, which made him a public figure and made her upbringing one of social and community awareness and responsibility.

As we got to know each other, Hadassah and I found we had a lot in common: strong family commitments to Jewish religious observance and values; childhoods full of opportunity in small, tolerant New England cities; and the painful lessons learned from failed marriages. Our values, personalities and priorities were much more clearly defined at age forty, which I was when I met Hadassah, who was then thirty-four. We each had a good sense of what we wanted in a life shared with a mate. She understood my life, as I did hers, and when I expressed my love ultimately by asking her to marry me, she answered not only with her love but with awareness of what our life together—public as well as private—would be like. We knew it would not always be easy, but we also knew that we were committed to each other and our shared values, and were confident we would work our way through the difficult times together.

In my campaign for attorney general, because I had been disappointed by my experience with national consultants in 1980, I hired only local consultants, including my pollster, Stan Greenberg, a New Haven friend and Yale political scientist, who ironically later became very national as pollster for Bill Clinton's winning 1992 presidential campaign. The incumbent Democratic attorney general ultimately retired, I received the nomination after a four-way contest, raised $200,000, and spent most of it telling the voters the ways in which I would fight for them as attorney general.

On election day 1982, I won a decisive victory, leading the state ticket in votes. I was particularly thrilled that I carried the congressional district I had lost just two years earlier—and by a very large margin. Father Dilion called again to say how thrilled he was that his faith and mine had been vindicated.

On March 20, 1983, Hadassah and I were married at my family's synagogue in Stamford. My time of political and personal defeat was behind me, I hoped. With lessons learned and a grateful appreciation for the opportunities I now had, I looked forward to beginning a new marriage and continuing my life of public service.

6

THE MODERN CAMPAIGN

DURING THE FALL of 1982, when I was running for attorney general, former vice president Walter Mondale came to Connecticut to speak to a Democratic dinner and told me the best job he ever had—better than senator or vice president—was attorney general of Minnesota. "When you are attorney general," Mondale explained, "all you do is sue the bastards, because by definition anyone the attorney general sues is a bastard."

Allowing a bit for Fritz Mondale's wit, he had a larger point, which was that the attorney general is inherently the people's lawyer, as I was promising to be in that campaign. He defends and enforces the values which the legislature and the courts have made into law. In Connecticut, where the attorney general has very little criminal jurisdiction, that particularly meant environmental and consumer protection, and human and civil rights enforcement. As Mondale had predicted, my six years as Connecticut's attorney general were some of the happiest and most satisfying of my life, a time when I came to fully appreciate and apply the principles I had learned at law school.

I was a very activist attorney general, taking air and water polluters to court, suing consumer rip-off artists, giving the damages I won back to consumers, representing the public at utility rate increase hearings and defending state laws, including one that protected workers' right to observe their religion and not suffer for it on the job, which I argued for before the U.S. Supreme Court. As the lawyer for state agencies, I became involved in a number of important and compelling cases that caused me to either issue opinions or go to court. One involved a disabled woman who became comatose after an accident and led to the first declaration by a Connecticut court of when life ends. But it was the consumer and environmental protection enforcement work that reinforced, from a different perspective, what I had learned as a state senator—that people need the protection of good laws or they will be cheated, polluted and otherwise taken advantage of by those who have more interest in profit or convenience than in doing what is fair and just. There is a relevant insight in the Babylonian Talmud:

"As it is with the fishes of the sea, the one that is larger swallows the others, so it is with humankind. Were it not for the fear of government, everyone greater than his fellow would 'swallow' him." (*Avodah Zara* 4a.)

My work as attorney general was very satisfying because my office was so often able to help some of those smaller fish. For example, I sued a New York–based finance company after receiving complaints from consumers who were shocked to learn that this company had placed second mortgages on their properties as part of home improvement work. My investigators found that thousands of middle- and lower-income families had been duped into signing documents that were second mortgages at exorbitant interest rates to finance vinyl siding, solar heating and other home improvements. In some cases, the signatures on the mortgaged documents appeared to be forged by the com-

pany's employees or agents. In federal district court, we obtained a settlement that gave more than three thousand
Connecticut homeowners the choice of having the second
mortgages removed and receiving cash payments of $1,400
or retaining the second mortgage and receiving larger cash
payments. It was a great victory that I know meant a lot to
those hardworking families.

During my time as attorney general, I found that environmental law enforcement work also had personal results.
Here again, I usually sued on behalf of people who did not
have the resources or capacity to protect themselves. There
were, for example, the families of Naugatuck, Connecticut,
who lived adjacent to a landfill with the lovely name Laurel
Park, which was not lovely at all. Their neighborhood was
constantly diminished by dump trucks on their way to the
park dropping garbage in front of their homes. And the residents had to use bottled water because their groundwater
was contaminated. We sued to stop the damage to the families and their neighborhood, and won.

In a different kind of environmental action, I went to
court to stop Springfield, Massachusetts, from dumping sew-
age into the Connecticut River, which would then flow into
our state.

Even some of the routine work of the Attorney General's office—like collections—took on special significance
when, for example, it came to collecting child-support debts
from delinquent fathers of children who were receiving state
assistance. As I studied my office's work in this area, and was
educated by Pat Caputo, a very impressive single mom who
had organized an advocacy group for better child-support
collection, I became outraged at the paternal irresponsibility.
I took my case to the Connecticut legislature, which gave my
office stronger collection laws. Then, I beefed up my child-

support division. The result was that we collected a lot more support money for the moms and kids and for the state.

Being attorney general was a full-time government job, which meant I could focus on my public responsibilities and better uphold my family responsibilities as well. I suddenly went from being a partner in a three-person private law firm to being "senior partner" in a public law firm of more than one hundred lawyers. There was superb talent within the Attorney General's office to help me manage and carry out my duties. Because this was my only job and because I was the "boss," I had much more control of my schedule than I did when I was a state senator and than I would when I became a U.S. senator. That was wonderful for the first years of my new marriage. I was busy, but when I left the house in the morning and told Hadassah the time I thought I would be returning, I was usually able to keep my promise. That is not so as a senator, where your schedule is determined by the Senate, its leaders' plans and your colleagues' rhetorical and amendatory inclinations.

While I went about my work as attorney general in Connecticut during the 1980s, I followed national politics closely and was especially fascinated by the enormous changes Ronald Reagan had brought to Washington. I was impressed by the strength, comfort, optimism and idealism that President Reagan radiated. His strong foreign and defense policies appealed to me greatly because they were so consistent with my personal opinions about America's role in the world, which were based on much reading of history and close attention to current events. President Reagan's emphasis on economic growth and the ease and skill with which he talked about fundamental American values also engaged me. I found his antigovernment rhetoric much less appealing because I retained a steadfast belief in the need for a good government—to maintain security, to increase opportunity and to provide for those who truly cannot provide for themselves. As I came to political maturity during the 1980s, President Reagan not only transformed his own party and our government but challenged many of us in the other party to decide where we would alter our views to accommodate the paradigm shift he had brought to our politics and where we would not. It was from such challenges and responses that the Democratic Leadership Council and the New Democratic movement were born in 1985 (I will have more to say about that later).

I ran for reelection as attorney general in 1986 on my record, and again led the state Democratic ticket, winning by 613,742 votes. Because state campaigns had become more centered on television advertising, which is expensive, I had to raise $440,000 for that 1986 campaign. When it ended victoriously, I began to set my sights four years forward when Governor Bill O'Neill was not expected to seek reelection, but a funny thing happened on the way to 1990. People started asking me to run against U.S. Senator Lowell Weicker in 1988.

Early in 1987, I took some of the money I had left over from my 1986 campaign and asked Stan Greenberg to do a post-election poll. He found two surprising results. In spite of my success as attorney general, I was running third behind two Democratic members of Congress in a matchup for my party's nomination for governor, and fewer than half the voters thought Senator Weicker deserved reelection. Stan suggested I think about running against Weicker. "You might win," he said, "but even if you don't, you will do better than most people think and raise your recognition statewide, so you will be a much stronger candidate for governor in 1990."

I can still see Hadassah and me and my campaign manager/executive assistant, Sherry Brown, in Stan's old office in New Haven and remember how stunned we were when he gave us those poll results and that advice. As I listened, my mind went back to a very different time and place. It was the fall of 1985, and I was sitting with my father at the family's kitchen table in Stamford. After fighting colon cancer for a year and a half, Pop, as my kids and I came to call him, was now clearly in the final weeks of his life, and my sisters, Rietta and Ellen, and I decided that each of us would spend every third night in Stamford, so one of us would always be with Pop and Mom, who refused all other offers of nursing assistance. Earlier that particular day I had lunch in Hartford with Peter Kelly, a local lawyer and national leader of the Democratic Party, who said I should think about running against Lowell Weicker in 1988. At the kitchen table that evening, I told Pop about the conversation. His face was already yellowed with jaundice and his voice was weak from medication, but he responded clearly: "You should think about it. Maybe people are ready for a change from Weicker, but even if you don't win, more people around the state will get to know you." A few months after that, on January 3, 1986, my father died. It was the most painful and, in its way, life-changing experience I had ever had. I had forgotten about our conversation concerning the Senate until Stan Greenberg gave me the same advice Pop had almost two years earlier.

The Democratic Party in Connecticut was having trouble in early 1987 finding a candidate to oppose Weicker because he looked so formidable. John Droney, the state chairman and a good friend, began to talk to me about it, arguing that I was in the fortunate position of having just been reelected to a four-year term as attorney general, so I could run for the Senate and not have to give up the position I had.

John told me he'd do everything he could to help me, as did many other people in the organization. There were other people urging me to run who, I suspected, were hoping I'd get beaten so badly by Weicker that I wouldn't be a credible candidate for governor in 1990. That, as they say, is politics.

Then I received a phone call from Senator John Kerry of Massachusetts. John and I had been undergraduate students at Yale together; he was a year behind me. He was now chairman of the national Democratic Senate Campaign Committee, which recruits and supports Democratic candidates for U.S. Senate seats across the country. The committee was particularly interested in Connecticut, where, with the 1988 elections approaching, they were looking for someone to run against Lowell Weicker. Kerry was calling to see if I was interested.

I thanked John, but asked him what was the case against Weicker. At first glance, the senator was a larger-than-life figure, a six-foot-six political maverick who had built his career on defying the status quo of his own party. As a freshman Republican senator on the committee investigating the Watergate scandal, Weicker had earned national exposure and a hero's reputation by denouncing President Nixon. He had continued to stand against his own party over the years on issues ranging from abortion (he was pro-choice) to the bombing of Libya (he strongly criticized President Reagan for that attack). I respected that kind of independence, although I sometimes disagreed with where it took Weicker, as in the criticism of Reagan for bombing Libya. But there was an arrogance about Weicker's independence that alienated many people, including a lot of Republicans.

Still, as I told Kerry, I needed more than Weicker's arrogance to base a campaign on. What was the message? How could I convince the voters to fire him and hire me? Kerry's response was to send me a thick book on Weicker's career, compiled by the Democratic Senate Campaign Committee. The book contained a detailed examination of Weicker's Senate voting record over the previous seventeen years, highlighting the issues and particular votes on which an opponent might focus. This was my first introduction to something that has become a staple of modern political campaigns: opposition research.

My staff and I had always tried to learn about my opponent's record in each of my previous political campaigns, but I had never seen anything so extensive and sophisticated as the study Kerry's committee sent me on Weicker. There was nothing personal in those pages, and I appreciated that. In the past decade or so, the business of opposition research has extended beyond public figures' professional performance and into their personal lives. Where at one time such research was conducted largely by campaign workers who focused exclusively on what the opponent had said and how he had voted, many candidates now hire private detectives to uncover "dirt" about their adversary. This mini-industry has proliferated to the point where these investigators—former police officers, former FBI agents, ex–CIA employees, former prosecutors and even ex-journalists—now have a name. They are called diggers.

As far as I am concerned, this kind of digging does nothing but demean our politics and defame the people who are its targets. There is nothing wrong with going after your opponent's voting record or any other evidence of negligence in his public life, but digging into his bank account, his phone records, his medical history, his sexual life and literally his garbage when these things have nothing to do with the performance of his public duties—past, present or future—is wrong.

That is how I looked at the Democratic book on Weicker. After reading it through, I was surprised by his bad voting record on several issues that strongly mattered to me, including environmental protection, foreign and defense policy and budget priorities like social security benefits. I also learned that he had missed a significant number of votes, including several to deliver speeches to private organizations that had legislation they were interested in before the Senate. The rules of the Senate have changed since then, but at that time a member was allowed to accept as much as $35,800 a year in honoraria as a guest speaker. The fact that Weicker had a record of missing votes in the Senate because he was delivering a speech to a lobbying organization from which he was personally paid a fee was outrageous and, I concluded, a fair issue to present to the voters.

This was a unique moment in my career. I had never been coy about having political ambitions and regularly thought about the next office I might seek. Ambition, when combined with principle, is one of the greatest sources of progress for a society—whether in business, the arts or politics. The challenge is to match your ambition, passion and talent with the right opportunity. In 1987, I was drawn into a race that I had not seriously considered, but it was for an office—United States senator—that was my ultimate ambition. During that summer we decided to take the next step and asked Stan Greenberg to do what politicians call a benchmark poll, a broad review of the candidates' popularity and of the public mood. At the same time, Hadassah and I began to talk seriously about what running for the Senate would mean to us personally. I remember joking in one of those conversations, "I have a job I love. We have a great life together. Why should we be satisfied with that?" Hadassah was understandably anxious, not so much about the demands of a Senate campaign but about what would happen to our lives if I got elected and we had to move to Washington, away from our families in Connecticut and New York. Then, late that July, our personal lives became more complicated when our prayers were answered and we learned that Hadassah was pregnant. We were thrilled, and, being traditionalists, we decided to keep the secret until later in the pregnancy.

Stan Greenberg was scheduled to come over to our house that Labor Day to report the results of his benchmark poll to Hadassah, Sherry Brown and me. Hadassah had continued to agitate about the decision, making pro-and-con lists on yellow lined legal paper, but early that morning, while we were out exercising, she told me she knew how important running for the Senate was, and if Stan brought encouraging poll results and I decided to run, she would do everything she could to help me. I was relieved, grateful and excited.

We sat in our kitchen that morning and listened to Stan's report—that this larger, longer poll had confirmed his two main earlier findings: Weicker was vulnerable; and I needed to raise my statewide recognition for whatever my future would be. I was twenty-five points behind Weicker in a head-to-head matchup, but the senator's "reelects" (the number of people who thought he deserved reelection) were in the low forties. Based on his sampling of Connecticut's mood, Stan then broadly outlined an unconventional strategy, which some commentators later called left-right. But Stan felt that it flowed naturally from my ideology, record and life. I would argue that Senator Weicker had stopped fighting for people in Connecticut in areas that mattered to them, such as environmental and consumer protection, where I had built a strong activist record as attorney general, but I would also discuss crime and foreign policy, where my beliefs were more conservative than Weicker's. Stan also said that I would be the candidate of traditional family values because that happened to be the way I lived. He turned then to Hadassah and joked, "If you really want to help this campaign, you will have a baby." We laughed hilariously, but the joke was on Stan, since we knew Hadassah was already pregnant.

Two months later, after I had decided to run, I called Stan and said, "Some candidates listen to their pollsters more than others. You remember you asked for a baby? Well, Stan, we're going to have a baby."

On March 15, 1988, Hana Rachel Lieberman was born. Named for my father, Henry, and Hadassah's aunt Rachel, Hana was and is a wondrous gift from God.

My decision to run for the Senate in 1988 meant mounting a campaign on a scale much broader and at a cost much greater than I had in my 1980 race for Congress and certainly in any of my campaigns for state office. This was my first taste of truly "national" politics, with support and guidance coming from the Democratic Senate Campaign Committee in Washington and with fund-raising efforts that needed to reach far beyond the borders of Connecticut. But the base of operations and control had to be within my state, with a first-rate staff that I trusted. In my very first campaign for the state senate, after trying for a few months to be both candidate and campaign manager, I realized you cannot do both well. A candidate needs to be free to think and act, without worrying about the details of campaign organization and management. Sherry Brown is a very smart, well-organized woman with business experience who walked into my headquarters to volunteer in the 1980 congressional campaign and never left. When I ran for attorney general, I asked her to become my paid campaign manager. When I was elected, she became my executive assistant. So in 1988,

I was lucky to have her ready and willing to run the campaign. She is the best.

Because I wanted my longtime press secretary, Jim Kennedy, to remain at the Attorney General's office to help me continue my work as "the people's lawyer" during the Senate campaign, I hired a separate campaign press secretary—Marla Romash, a Connecticut journalist who had previously worked for Senator Chris Dodd. Jimmy O'Connell, a very able and gregarious New Haven policeman who had been my volunteer driver for eighteen years and become one of my best friends, would be my aide-de-camp on the trail. As Jimmy once modestly summed up our roles: "You concentrate on war and peace, feast and famine. I'll make sure we get to the next stop." Sherry Brown then went about hiring other needed personnel, including state and national fundraisers.

The choice of media consultants was difficult and fascinating. First, I learned that there were Democratic media firms and Republican media firms, and rarely did the twain meet. When I called one firm whose television commercials for a Republican presidential candidate I had admired, I was told politely that the firm worked only for Republicans. After considering several of the Democratic consulting groups, which meant interviewing the principals, viewing and listening to their work and speaking with past clients, we chose Bob Squier, one of the most respected professionals in the field. When Bob turned our campaign "account" over to his young associate, Carter Eskew, whom I had never heard of, I was disappointed. But Carter, a Yale graduate who had been a reporter for the *Nashville Tennessean* (along with Al Gore) and for the *Village Voice* in New York City before working in political campaigns in that state, soon became the creative heart of my campaign and a very good friend besides. Squier

stayed involved, particularly in filming our campaign commercials.

I set about studying domestic and international issues
and securing Connecticut Democratic political support with
enthusiasm and pleasure. Fund-raising was another matter.
I've always had difficulty asking people for money. In earlier
campaigns it had taken me a long time to become comfortable calling people I knew in Connecticut, although in the
end I always managed to raise enough money. But now I had
to call people I didn't know all across the country. I felt awk-
ward. I knew it was necessary, that indeed the first stage of
any campaign at this level is the "financial primary"—you've
got to raise enough money by the time you file your first
financial report (which was due December 31, 1987) to demonstrate that you're a viable candidate. But I still felt uncomfortable with it. I would think of my dad and his ethic of
self-reliance, working so hard in that liquor store so that his
kids would never have to ask for anything, sending us to college without asking for scholarships or financial aid, always
paying his way and ours. I had no trouble getting on the
phone and asking for money for a charity or for somebody
else, but asking for myself was very hard, very unnatural.

I shared this feeling early on at a meeting in Washington in late 1987 of Democratic Senate candidates from
across the country with Democratic senators. I remember
being questioned hard—essentially interrogated—by members of the Senate about my reluctance to raise money. Tom
Daschle, the senator from South Dakota and now the Senate's minority leader, finally said to me, "Let me be blunt
with you, Joe. To have a chance to win, you've got to be able
to get your message to the public, mostly on television. To
get on television, you've got to have money to buy the advertising. And to have the money, you've got to be able to raise

it. If you're finding it hard to ask people for money," he concluded, "then you'd better not run." He was right. I went home and got on the phone, beginning with my family and Connecticut friends, from whom I raised a very respectable $367,000 by the first reporting deadline.

The equation of money and television in American political campaigns today cannot be overstated. If there is one factor that has most dramatically altered our political landscape since I entered politics thirty years ago, it is the power of TV. There is no doubt about its scope (though not necessarily its depth) and effectiveness as a vehicle of exposure and communication, which explains why the focus of almost every political campaign at almost every level of government in our country today is on television advertising. Television can move voters just as it can move consumers of cars, creams or candy.

Television was hardly a factor when I entered politics at the state level in 1970. By the time I ran for Congress in 1980 and for state attorney general in 1982, TV advertising had become an integral part of my campaigns. But none of those experiences compared to the extent, the expense and the impact television advertising had when I ran for that U.S. Senate seat in 1988. That was my personal introduction to the big-time campaign financing on a national scale which is necessary to pay for local TV time.

One of the first things I had to learn about was PACs (political action committees), which were created by the post-Watergate campaign finance reform laws. These are groups of like-minded people—doctors, plumbers, teachers, realtors—who pool their individual political contributions and then give to a particular candidate whom the PAC naturally hopes or expects will support its interests. By law, no candidate can receive more than $10,000 from a PAC in each election cycle and all contributions are publicly disclosed. When I decided to run for the Senate in late 1987, people told me I would have trouble raising money from any PACs because most of these groups give most of their contributions to incumbents, since incumbents are not only known commodities but likely winners. A small number of PACs contribute to both candidates in an election, ensuring a connection of support no matter who wins. But even these groups tended to shy away from me in my race against Weicker because I was a long shot and he had a long memory. As one PAC executive told me during 1988: "We would love to help you win, but we can't take a chance on you because the odds are Weicker will be reelected, and when he sees our name on your report, he will be brutal to us. If you win, we'll help you wipe out your deficit." Thanks a lot, I thought. If I win the election, everybody will help me pay my bills. But I need it now.

Even toward the end of the campaign, when I closed in on Weicker in the public polling and people began to think I might have a chance, most of the PACs continued to play it safe and gave me nothing. Even the pro-Israel PACs shunned me. One of the most frustrating, eye-opening experiences of the 1988 campaign was approaching several largely Jewish, pro-Israel PACs and finding that they had a hard-and-fast rule of not giving any support to challengers facing incumbents with a pro-Israel voting record, no matter who the challenger was or what his stance on Israel. Weicker had a pro-Israel record, so I was shut out. In some cities, I couldn't even get individual donations from members of these PACs. That's how strict they were. The one contribution I received in that campaign from a pro-Israel PAC came from a group in New Jersey, and I will always believe that was only because a cousin of mine was the treasurer. I don't think he told anyone else in the group that he wrote that check until after the election.

The bulk of my fund-raising came from individual donations from people in Connecticut and across the country. Much as I went door-to-door during my first state senate campaign back in 1970, I began crisscrossing the country early in 1988, raising money at office and home visits, breakfast and lunch meetings, cocktail receptions and dinners in America's major cities. My targets were people who had given before to Democratic Senate candidates. I made progress, but it wasn't quick or easy. I remember telling a friend that sometimes on the fund-raising trail I felt like Willy Loman in *Death of a Salesman*. I have never been through anything in my professional life as physically and mentally demanding as that 1988 campaign. It was uphill all the way, like a marathon—learning issues, speaking at events, trying to get so-called free media (news coverage in Connecticut of what I was doing and saying), and raising money, raising money, raising money. With all these demands on me, I came to understand how important stamina—sheer physical and intellectual stamina—is to a political candidate. It's important to be informed, personable, creative, well advised and well supported, but none of those things is going to get you where you want to go if you haven't got the stamina to endure the day-to-day mental and physical pressure of a modern-day political campaign. If you are interested in a political career, I can tell you right now you had better stay in shape.

Los Angeles was an important fund-raising target for us in that 1988 campaign because two of the largest groups of traditional donors to Democrats are members of the film and television industry and members of the Jewish community, both of which are concentrated in the L.A. area. But Weicker was very popular with both these groups, as I found out when I got there. My national fund-raiser, Norman Kurz, was with me as too many meetings ended with the two of us leaving someone's office with friendly handshakes but no check.

After one of these sessions, with the leader of a pro-Israel PAC who had explained why they couldn't support me, I decided to step outside for some fresh air. Norman stayed behind to make a few phone calls. It was a typically gorgeous Southern California day, and I noticed a small grassy area across the street. I said to myself, "The hell with it, I might as well get some sun out of this trip." So I strolled over, took off my jacket and lay down on that soft lawn in the warmth of the sun.

Norman finished his calls, walked outside and couldn't find me. He went back in, brought out the man we'd come to see, and they both began looking around. Suddenly Norman saw me lying on the ground across the street and said, "Oh my God. He's *killed* himself."

Sometimes it almost seemed that bad. But when all was said and done, we were able to raise a very impressive total of $2.6 million, which was only slightly less than Weicker raised, and was enough to enable me to get my message out on television. That total shows that while incumbents clearly have a built-in fund-raising advantage, challengers—even those like me, without either personal wealth or the probability of winning—*can* raise enough money to be competitive.

How did we do it? In 1987 and 1988 my fund-raising efforts benefited from a strong economy. Potential contributors had disposable income. The centers of my fund-raising were naturally in Connecticut, where I had developed a strong core of contributors and was assisted by the Democratic organization, and in New York, because it was just next door and had a lot of traditional Democratic contributors among its business leaders and a large Jewish population whose ethnic identification with me was a plus.

The fact that I was the attorney general gave me legitimacy and recognition and certainly made it easier to raise money in Connecticut and, at least once, outside the state. After the campaign was over, the CEO of a New York investment banking company told me that when I had called him a few months earlier and his secretary announced that Attorney General Lieberman of Connecticut was on the phone, he put me on hold and frantically called his general counsel. "What have we done wrong in Connecticut?" he demanded. The lawyer didn't know. When the CEO learned that all I wanted was a campaign contribution, he was so relieved he told me he'd send a thousand dollars, even though, as he admitted later, he never heard my name before.

With all that, our budget got so tight during the closing weeks of that campaign, when Weicker and I were running neck and neck and we needed to keep buying television time, that Hadassah and I did something we had never done before—and will never do again. We opened a $100,000 line of credit with a lien on our house to help finance the ads we knew we would need for the stretch run of that campaign.

When that race had begun, in the fall of 1987, our polling showed I was twenty-five points behind Weicker. Sometimes I look back and wonder how I even ran, when I was starting in such a deep hole. My strategy, developed with Carter Eskew, was to open in the spring of 1988 with a series of television ads introducing myself and framing my central message to the voters, which was that Lowell Weicker was

no longer representing the interests of the people of Connecticut so much as he was representing himself and his own
interests. I would fight for them in Washington as I had in
Hartford as their attorney general. Carter inverted Weicker's
traditional slogan, "Nobody's Man but Yours," into a tag
line—"Nobody's Man but Whose?"—which ran after commercials describing votes the senator had cast against the environment, consumers or popular social programs.

While I punched away at him throughout the spring
and summer, Weicker ignored me. Other than one debate in
the summer, he treated me as if I was not worth bothering
with. Early in the fall, it seemed that his strategy was working. We had only cut that twenty-five-point lead to sixteen. I
remember having a conversation with Carter and asking him
what in the world was going on here. I felt that we were
doing everything right. In extensive television advertising
and personal appearances in pursuit of news coverage around
the state, we were really distinguishing between Weicker and
me, yet I was still so far behind. What was going on? In a
piece of true wisdom, Carter said, "You know, it could be
that the public is just so fixed on this guy, they've got him so
much in their embrace—from Watergate, from his image,
from his incumbency—that they'll never let him go.

"Or," he continued, "on the other hand, it could be that
every time we put one of these ads on about his voting
record, we're making people think, and their embrace is
loosening a little bit more every time, and finally, all it will
take is one thing to happen, and they'll just let him go."

That October, the one thing did happen. Back in the
spring my campaign team and I had had a brainstorming session, framing our thoughts on a variety of policy and political
matters. At one point we were talking about Weicker himself, and Carter asked, "What do you see when you think of

Weicker? What image comes to mind?" My answer was a
bear—a big, lumbering bear who comes out of his cave now
and then and growls for a while, then goes back in and you
don't hear from him for a couple of months. The rest of us
forgot the conversation, but Carter kept that image in mind
all summer, and now, he decided, it was time to use it, to
build a television commercial around it. The brilliant thing
Carter did was rather than make a straight-ahead serious
spot, he produced a satire, using a cartoon in which Weicker
was portrayed as a sleeping bear. The element of light
humor, along with the razor-sharp point that this senator was
missing votes to accept honoraria, apparently struck a chord
because in the middle of October the *Hartford Courant* ran
the stunning results of its own poll under a memorable banner headline: "Dead Heat." We were now neck and neck.

At that point Weicker stopped ignoring me. He hit back
with a barrage of attack commercials, portraying me the
same way Larry DeNardis had back in 1980—as a big-taxing
big spender. One of those ads was technically accurate but
didn't mention that the tax votes cited were cast seventeen
years earlier, in 1971. My son Matt saw Weicker's television
commercials and said to me when I came home after a long,
exhausting day of campaigning, "Dad, if you weren't my father and I saw those ads, I wouldn't vote for you." I remem-
bered 1980 and immediately called Sherry, Carter and Stan;
they went into the field with a poll the next day that showed
the negative ads were killing me. In that private poll I had
gone from dead even to nine points behind—in one week.

That was when Hadassah and I took out the note on
our house. The fact that we had drawn even in the public
newspaper polling, however, prompted an eleventh-hour
rush of contributions, and—thank God—we never had to use
that line of credit. The extra money enabled us to answer

Weicker's attacks, and the campaign finished with toe-to-toe dueling television commercials about who had done, and would do, more for Connecticut's people.

When I had decided to run in 1988, I knew the odds were against my winning, but I thought I had a chance. If I lost, I hoped I would at least improve my recognition in the state. My one great fear was that I would suffer a humiliating defeat that would leave me better known, but as a loser. As election day neared, the polls and the people I met made me confident that even if victory was not to be had, humiliation would not happen either. That gave me a nothing-to-lose confidence in the two debates Weicker and I had during that time which helped me do very well.

There were two other unusual factors in the atmosphere of that campaign. One was my Republican support, and the other was my religious observance. Some prominent Republicans, who had become disenchanted or infuriated with Senator Weicker and were coincidentally personal friends of mine, publicly endorsed me. Among the most visible were Pat Sullivan, who had led the Reagan-for-President movement in Connecticut in 1980; Dick Bozzuto, my former state senate colleague and Republican candidate for governor; and, most interestingly, Bill Buckley, the intellectual leader of the modern American conservative movement and a friend through our shared love for the *Yale Daily News*. Buckley formed BuckPAC, whose declared purpose was to remove Lowell Weicker from the Senate, and announced that membership was open only to anyone in Connecticut named Buckley. I remember telling Bill at the time that he was playing a rabbinical role in the campaign by effectively telling the conservative Republicans in the state who didn't like Weicker that "Joe Lieberman is a kosher alternative."

My personal religious observance became more public

than it had ever been before because it occasionally inter-
sected with the campaign schedule in ways that were visible
and aroused a good deal of journalistic interest. For instance,
I did not attend the state Democratic convention which nom-
inated me because it was held, by tradition, on a Saturday, and
I had long ago decided that I would not participate in purely
political activities on the Sabbath. However, modern technology allowed me to pre-record an acceptance speech.

Sometimes, during that campaign, people would ask me
what I would do if there were votes or important meetings in
the Senate on the Sabbath. I told them I distinguished between political events and governmental responsibilities that
affected people's well-being or safety. In the latter case, I believed I had not just a political but a religious responsibility
to act, even on the Sabbath. So as a senator, I would vote or
attend sessions held on Saturday.

On the Thursday before that 1988 election, I received a
call from my friend Cornelius O'Leary, the Democratic
leader of the Connecticut state senate, who told me that he
now thought I was going to win the election. I said I was naturally glad to hear that, but why did he *now* think I would
win? I'll never forget his answer.

"I went to visit my mother's house yesterday afternoon,"
he said, "and she had four of her friends over for tea. I asked
them who they were going to support for president next
Tuesday. They all said Bush. I made the case for [Michael]
Dukakis but couldn't convince any of them.

"Then I asked about the Senate, and my mother said,
'That's easy. I'm voting for Joe Lieberman.'

"I asked, 'Why is that so easy?'

" 'Because,' my mother responded, 'I like the fact that
Joe Lieberman is a religious man.'

"At that," O'Leary said, "the other women at the table

nodded. So Joe, I now think your religious observance, which I thought might hurt you because it requires you to miss so many days of campaigning, will actually help elect you. It tells people that something matters to you more than political success. My mother and her friends are Christian, and you're Jewish, but the fact that you so clearly share their belief in God gives them a personal bond with you."

On the day before the election, in the last public event of that campaign, we went to my mother's house in Stamford to sit with her, Hadassah and our four children, including our wonderful new daughter, Hana, to talk about the values I had learned in that house, values I promised to bring to Washington if elected. During a particularly serious part of my remarks, Hana, who was sitting on my lap, burped. I reflexively moved my hand to cover her mouth, and made a hilariously shocked face. The *Hartford Courant* photographer caught the moment, and the paper ran the adorable (if I may say so) picture on election morning, under the caption "The Baby Burped."

When the 1,383,516 votes were finally counted late that night, I had won a most improbable victory, by just 10,043 votes—less than one percent of the total. Hadassah and I decided that the captivating election day picture of the baby had provided the margin of victory and told Hani, when she was old enough to understand, that it was her burp that elected me to the United States Senate.

Maybe it was a little bit more than Hani's burp. The 1988 campaign had been the biggest test of my public life. I was blessed with steadfast support from my wife and family, and received extraordinary help from people throughout the state. But I had to raise what was for me then an enormous amount of money. I had to work with my staff and professional consultants to structure a message that grew out of my work as the attorney general but also extended to cover national and international issues on which I had not previously spoken. And I had to remain tactically alert and agile as the campaign twisted and turned. All of which is to say that in 1988, I really learned how to run a modern political campaign. I hope my 1988 campaign encourages people who are thinking of getting into politics, because it shows how open our political system can be to new candidates with different ideas. It also illustrates the willingness of the voters to listen to the candidates' vision for the future and to assess the values they would bring to their public service. I had to demonstrate the differences between Senator Weicker and me in order to have a chance to go to Washington to make a difference, so I presented a clear set of priorities and promises: to stimulate economic growth, to pursue strong, internationalist defense, economic and foreign policies, to protect the environment and to uphold and advance broadly held values that grow out of America's shared faith. As I prepared to leave for Washington, I felt very lucky to have the opportunity ahead to pursue those priorities and try to keep those promises.

7

THE LIFE

AFTER MY UPSET ELECTION to the Senate, I was inundated with congratulations, advice and new friends. But perhaps the best advice I received came from an old friend, Archbishop John Whalen of the Catholic Diocese of Hartford. Before going to Washington, I made private visits to three religious leaders who meant a lot to me, to ask them for their prayers as I began this new chapter of my life: the Lubavitch rabbi Menachem Schneerson in Brooklyn, New York, who had long been an inspiration to me; the Reverend Ken Fellenbaum, an Evangelical minister, supporter and friend from Milford, Connecticut; and Archbishop Whalen at his residence in Hartford. The archbishop gave me one piece of advice I had not expected. "Leave time for solitude, Joe," he told me. "Make space for thinking and reading." I had no idea then how wise the archbishop's counsel was.

When I arrived in Washington as a newly elected senator, I attended a series of orientation seminars for incoming freshmen, including one in which Alan Simpson, then senator from Wyoming, spoke about the dangers of senatorial overload. He told us how he had arrived on Capitol Hill years before, an ardent newcomer just as we were. Every day

his schedule was crammed from dawn to dark with meetings
(committee meetings, meetings with staff, meetings with colleagues, meetings with constituents), with speeches to make
(at breakfasts, lunches and dinners), with press interviews
(from newspapers and magazines and radio and television),
with receptions (at cocktail parties, social events, cultural
performances). Every night he would trudge home with
enough paperwork to break a packhorse's back, as he put it.
Then he would rise the next morning to do it all over again.
Eager, resolute, anxious to make his mark, he kept up this
pace for about three months, he said, until he finally realized
he was about to fall apart. At that point he called his staff together, sat them down and made an announcement. "Regarding my schedule," he told them, "I just want to remind
you of one thing: If I die, you're all out of work."

This is a common syndrome in any profession: the new
employee eager to prove to others and to himself how well
he can do his job. There is nothing wrong with such zeal, but
at some point you have to learn to draw lines, to make
choices, to understand that you can't do it all, and shouldn't.

I understood Simpson's advice, I knew exactly what he
meant . . . and I promptly proceeded to ignore it. Since it
was the middle of the school year when I began my new job
during January 1989, Hadassah stayed in Connecticut so
Ethan—then thirteen—could finish eighth grade. Meanwhile I moved into a college friend's vacant apartment for six
months and, having nothing but my work to do, I did exactly
what Simpson had warned against. I worked myself to death.
Beyond the necessary duties that took up almost my entire
day, I accepted every invitation possible, attended every re-
ception I could, made the optional almost a requirement, and
was up until well past midnight each evening reading and

studying the paperwork I'd lugged home. It didn't take me long to realize that this was not the most effective way to be a senator. First, like Simpson, I soon understood that at this rate I was going to kill myself. And secondly, when you are a politician in a city like Washington, there are *always* invitations, every night, to events and gatherings that can seem alluringly fascinating, occasionally glamorous and possibly important, and are actually often pleasant, and sometimes even worthwhile. But the trade-off for your own precious time and energy is a high price to pay, and you quickly learn to pick and choose these invitations carefully.

I'll never forget getting an invitation from Ted Stevens, the senator from Alaska, to attend a dinner he and his wife, Cathy, were hosting at their home in honor of Warren Rudman, the senator from New Hampshire. Rudman, whose office was fortunately right next to mine, became a mentor to me. He was a notorious recluse when it came to evening events. He never went out at night. "It's a waste of time," he told me once. "I can't take it. I go home and read books."

When I saw Stevens on the Senate floor the next day, I told him I'd gotten the invitation and that Hadassah and I would love to come. "But what's the occasion?" I asked him. "Is it Warren's birthday?"

"Oh, no, no," he said. "The dinner is in honor of Warren because he's agreed to come."

Ted Stevens's comment made me laugh, but it also made me think. In spite of the extremes to which Warren Rudman went to protect his private time, he was widely regarded as a superb senator, one of the best. That confirmed what I had learned during my madcap first six months in Washington, which is that a lot of what I was spending my time on did nothing to make me a better senator for my state or country.

Besides, my wife and infant child had come to live in Washington with me, and I wanted to spend time with them.

When you're elected to Congress, you suddenly work in a place where you don't live, or to put it another way, you suddenly live in two places. "When you're a senator," one of my colleagues once glumly said to me, "home is where you're not." One of the first decisions you have to make is whether you are going to bring your family to Washington with you. I remember one of my Senate colleagues who had come to Washington married, and after a few years with his wife living in his home state, got divorced, advising me: "You don't appreciate it now, Joe," he said, "but this is where you work. You're going to spend as much as three-quarters of your time here, and if you leave your wife in Connecticut, it will just not be good for your marriage." He was right, and we decided that Hadassah and Hani, who was then barely a year old, would move to Washington in June 1989.

Another thing that surprised me when I first arrived in the capital was how many of my colleagues in the Senate do not own residences in their home states because they also want their families with them in Washington and can't afford to own two homes. The annual salary of a U.S. senator in 1989 was $89,500—not enough to maintain two mortgages. Today it is $141,300, a lot of money for most Americans, but by itself still not enough to easily pay for two homes, at least not when one of them is in as expensive a city as Washington. John Rowland, a former congressman and now governor of Connecticut, called me after the 1988 election and said, "Congratulations, you now live in two of the most expensive real estate markets in America at the same time." What some of my colleagues do once they are elected is sell their house in their home state and maintain their legal residence there with a family member or friend.

For me, this was a dilemma. First, my family and I were very attached to our home and neighbors in New Haven. They were our dearest friends. Some of them were members of our synagogue and Sabbath Bible-study group, and were with us at our times of greatest personal joy and sadness. Our Connecticut friends were friends before I became a senator and would be friends after. We didn't want to cut ourselves off from them or from the city of New Haven, which I had loved since I arrived at Yale in 1960. I was also politically sensitive about not having a house in Connecticut and opening myself to accusations by an opponent of "going Washington" and abandoning my roots. But that's what Hadassah and I might have been forced to do if it had not been for help from our family that enabled us to live in a townhouse in the Burleith section of Washington and still keep our home in New Haven.

After we married in 1983, Hadassah had for a time continued her career in health care consulting and public relations, commuting a few days a week to New York from our home in Connecticut. But that became difficult, so she began working part-time in New Haven. When we came to Washington, she wanted to work, and we needed the additional income. Having a full- or part-time job was a relative rarity for senators' wives a generation ago but is much more common today. The role of spouses in public life has changed over the past thirty years in much the same way the role of spouses in all walks of life has changed. Politically and independently active spouses such as Eleanor Roosevelt were an extreme exception until the 1970s. A wife's role—and they were almost always wives, since the politicians were almost always men— was to support and encourage her husband's career while taking care of her home and family. During the First World War a group of wives, calling themselves the Ladies of the

Senate, began meeting once a week to roll bandages for the war effort and then have lunch together. When Hadassah arrived in Washington, this group was still meeting, but their number was smaller. Many of the wives—and husbands (the group is now called Spouses of the Senate)—didn't have the time. Most of them had jobs and careers of their own. Hadassah would try hard not to miss the weekly lunches of this group because she enjoyed the company and derived comfort and counsel from the only women in Washington who were living pretty much the same life she was.

When Hadassah began looking for a job in Washington, we both agreed to be careful about avoiding anything that might appear to be a conflict of interest. We both wanted her to pursue her own career as independently as possible from mine. But we found, as she began to interview for jobs, that prospective employers were more interested in entertaining or employing her as Senator Lieberman's wife than as an independent, capable, experienced candidate for a job. Others were worried about how much work she would miss when she returned to Connecticut with me. After several weeks of elegant lunch meetings with no offers she could accept, Hadassah told me, "At this rate, I'm going to get fat before I get a job."

She finally did find appropriate employment, first with the National Research Council, building private sector support for better math and science education, and then as a consultant with a public affairs firm that agreed to protect her from conflicts of interest. She worked only for nonprofit organizations and did no lobbying. In the last few years, as our daughter Hani, who is now eleven, has grown older, Hadassah has begun working part-time out of our home as a women's health care consultant, so we can all spend more time together.

This gets back to the warning Alan Simpson issued when I first came to Washington, and it's a challenge to anyone in any career. Balancing one's job and one's life is tremendously difficult. But it is also tremendously essential.

Once, Hadassah and I were talking about how being a senator might change a person, and she warned, "Remember, being a senator is just your job. It's not you." She was so right. Being a senator is a great job, a great honor and a great opportunity, but it is, after all, just my job. When a senator begins to think of himself only as "The Senator," he is on the road to trouble. Coming to Washington with children, particularly an infant, helped keep me from inhaling the intoxicating aura of the capital, as I know it does for all my colleagues who are parents. There is nothing like coming home and changing a baby's diaper to remind you that "being a senator is just your job." The presence of children in the house also creates a pull—some might call it guilt—that helps members of Congress go home and thereby avoid getting stretched thin by their work schedules.

When Hadassah heard that Hillary Clinton was thinking of running for the U.S. Senate from New York, she said, "I just don't understand why she'd want a job where she has to wait at the end of the day until the Senate majority leader tells her she can go home." That is the voice of a spouse who has kept dinner in the oven too many nights, waiting for my Senate colleagues to stop speaking and for the Senate leaders to agree there would be no more votes so we could go home. In fact, a lot of us try to live close enough to the Capitol that we can go home for dinner to see our families and still be able to rush back when the cloakroom staff calls to say a vote is about to occur.

Now add to this busy life in Washington the fact that it is not home. We live in Connecticut and want and need to be there, too, with our family, friends and constituents. Before air-conditioning (which enables Congress to stay in session during the torrid Washington summer) and airplanes (which enable us to leave the capital and return quickly), members of Congress would come to Washington in January, stay in session for several months and then go home for several months. No more. Today we are all in varying degrees of constant motion between Washington, our home states and, when we are in reelection cycle, other places around the country for campaign fund-raising. I am lucky because the planes make the relatively short trip to Connecticut or nearby New York airports very frequently and quickly. Many of my colleagues have to allot the better part of a day for westward travel.

When our daughter Hani was younger, our family would go home to New Haven two or even three weekends a month. Now, since she is in school in D.C. and has friends there, we don't want to pull her out too often, so we go together to New Haven for one weekend a month, as well as for the summer recess and holidays. I make the trip several other days a month by myself. And when we are all in Washington together, Hadassah and I try not to go out more than one night a week. Because we have three grown children, we know how quickly Hani's childhood will be over, and we don't want to miss it.

In the helter-skelter push and pull of Senate life, Hadassah and I have found that our religious observances provide very welcome relief, particularly the Sabbath, that weekly sanctuary between sunset on Friday and sundown on Saturday. This is the time when the worldly concerns of the rest of the week are put on hold so that we can focus on appreciating all that God has given us. It is a day apart, when my family and I are able to reconnect with one another and with our spiritual selves, to pray, to talk, to read, to rest or to just plain enjoy ourselves. It is a "time beyond time," as one rabbi called it. In fact, I usually don't wear a watch on the Sabbath. I treasure that time, twenty-four hours with no meetings, no telephone calls, no television, no radio, no traveling, no business of any sort. My Connecticut Senate colleague, Chris Dodd, once joked with me that he would consider converting to Judaism just for the weekends.

As I promised during my campaign for the Senate in 1988, when there are meetings or votes on the Sabbath that affect people's health, well-being or security, I have attended. For me, this is consistent with rabbinic opinions that have, for instance, instructed doctors that they *must* ignore specific prohibitions of the Sabbath (such as not using a phone, a car or electricity) to protect someone's health or life. That certainly makes sense since the purpose of the Sabbath is to honor and appreciate God's creation. How, then, could we allow technical rules of Sabbath observance to stop us from protecting God's greatest creation—people?

In my eleven years in Washington, I have attended crisis meetings at the White House three or four times on Saturdays and the Senate has been in session twenty-five or thirty times on the Sabbath. My colleagues want to be with their families or constituents on Friday night and Saturday so, when we're at the Capitol, it is for something important, like the Gulf war debate, the federal budget crises of 1990 and 1995 or the impeachment trial of President Clinton. On those occasions I have tried hard to fulfill my responsibility to the public without violating the specific rules that have been established over the centuries to protect the Sabbath as a day of rest, and make it different. For example, if we are meeting on both Friday night and Saturday, I will stay at a hotel near the Capitol, usually with Hadassah and Hani to avoid driving a car. If we're meeting on only one of those days, I'll walk the four miles between our home and the Capitol. Particularly when these walks are at night, the Capitol police provide me with an escort, on foot and in an accompanying car, which has led me to wish my European immigrant grandmother, Baba, could see me.

My Senate colleagues, just like my Connecticut constituents, have been not just tolerant but very respectful of my religious observance, which I truly appreciate. On my very first Sabbath at the Capitol, in 1989, before I had the routine down, I was planning to sleep on a cot in the Senate gym until Al Gore insisted I stay at his parents' apartment across the street. When I see Al's wonderful mother, Pauline, she always calls me her "tenant." During the impeachment trial, my Senate colleague Slade Gorton of Washington graciously offered to host Hadassah, Hani and me in his Capitol Hill home. And a Sabbath in the Senate never passes without Barbara Mikulski of Maryland coming over to say, in pretty good Polish-American Yiddish, "Good Shabbos, Joey."

On every other day of the week, it is Jewish tradition to pray three times—morning, afternoon and evening. The afternoon service is, for me, the most difficult to stop for because it is in the middle of the workday. That is also why it is most important. So I have put a small prayer book next to the phone on the desk in my Senate office to remind me to pause and enjoy the perspective and calm that prayer offers. It definitely eases my way through the day.

For many members of Congress, religious observance also provides the most significant nonpolitical communities we belong to in Washington. The members of our churches and synagogues, like our neighbors and the parents of our children's schoolmates, become our second-home communities away from our communities in our home states or dis-

tricts and make our lives in Washington richer than just a re-
volving door at the Capitol.

One of the worst consequences of the hectic lives senators lead is that we don't see enough of each other away from
work. That is a shame because, believe it or not, senators are
a very interesting and enjoyable group to spend time with.
They are naturally affable, or they wouldn't be in politics.
Sometimes people will ask me who are my best friends in the
Senate. I always begin my answer with Chris Dodd, but after
that it depends on which of the other senators our schedule
has allowed or forced me to spend the most time with in recent weeks. In the old days, when members of Congress
came to Washington for months at a time, they and their
families would socialize with one another on weekends. Almost none of that happens now. Since the pace of work was
slower then, members also took the time to gather at the end
of the day for social drinks. That rarely happens anymore. In
fact, there is very little drinking by members of the Senate
today, alone or together. Since much of the bygone family
and collegial socializing naturally crossed party lines, I am
sure it helped avoid some of the rancorous and destructive
partisanship that erupts too often today.

But there are still two good times I have found to get to
know my colleagues personally. One is when we have traveled to foreign countries and spent extended time in close
quarters together. The other is the weekly Senate prayer
breakfast, at which about twenty or thirty current and former
senators gather privately in a room at the Capitol each
Wednesday morning with our chaplain, Lloyd Ogilvie, for
prayer, reflection and conversation. This is the place and
time in the Capitol that has felt most like home to me, when
party affiliation is irrelevant and we speak of our faith, experience, priorities and concern for one another.

I remember once reading a description of Washington as America's temple of power, where senators are the high priests. That, of course, is greatly overstated, as the pace of our lives suggests, but the capital can be a very seductive and ego-inflating place. Senators are given much respect and deference, and run the risk of being misguided by this attention. Doors are opened for us; good seats at sporting and entertainment events and restaurants are easily obtained. Wealthy and famous people entertain us. Sometimes you've got to remind yourself who you are and why you wanted to be there. If you don't, the odds are that the media and your constituents eventually will.

I would guess that one of the most prevalent public misconceptions of the "seductive" life of members of Congress in Washington, particularly in the aftermath of the Lewinsky scandal, concerns their sexual excesses and infidelities. It may be happening more than I think, but I just haven't seen very much of it among my colleagues. That probably has a lot to do with the fact that the freedom politicians of earlier eras had to pursue private sexual relationships while the press looked the other way is now a thing of the distant past. Ask Gary Hart, or President Clinton.

As far as elected officials using their position of power to take advantage of women, that has changed too. First, women have thankfully become more self-protective and assertive than they were a generation ago; they simply won't stand for such behavior. And they have the law to support them. Any senator who might be thinking of chasing a staff member around his desk or planting a kiss on her lips need only be reminded of Bob Packwood to think again.

I am, of course, not saying that there is no sexual misconduct in Washington, but I would guess that the level of such activity is less among the group of men and women with whom I work on Capitol Hill than among a random group of 535 people in most other jobs in our society. People in public life are as full of frailties and vulnerabilities as anyone else, but their lives are lived today in a context of microscopic scrutiny that does not compare to the relative freedom and privacy they enjoyed a generation ago and that most other people in our society still enjoy. The fear of personal mortification, career destruction and emotional devastation for family and friends is a powerful deterrent for any public figure who is tempted to pursue an immoral relationship.

I have tried in this chapter to describe through my own experiences the impact that public life has on the private lives of people in politics, and how my family and I have worked hard to separate the two. It does take work, because public life is time-consuming and all-encompassing, and can be uniquely intrusive unless you protect your privacy and do not behave in a way that encourages media or political intrusion. But I remain convinced that the opportunities for making a difference that come with *public* life are worth the efforts that are necessary to protect the *rest* of your life.

8

THE JOB

ON A RECENT VISIT to an elementary school in Connecticut, a fifth grader asked me a direct and unexpected question: "Do you like your job?" My unrehearsed answer was: "I love my job. Of course, like all jobs, sometimes it's boring and sometimes it's frustrating. And it's not an easy job. But I love it because every day I go to work knowing I will meet interesting people, learn new things and have a chance to do something about important problems."

That pretty much sums it up. Now let me fill in the details.

When you come to the Senate, you bring the experience and knowledge you have accumulated during your life— which is necessarily limited. Yet you are expected to make judgments and laws across a very broad spectrum of human experience and knowledge. To do that well, you must leave time to listen to the people who live or work in the fields where you are legislating. And you must hire the best, most experienced staff you can find. I have tried to do the former, and have been lucky, regarding the latter, to have brilliant, effective and committed staff in both my Washington and Hartford offices.

Then, you should prioritize, but that's not easy because

there are so many compelling and critical issues before the Senate, and the brilliant, effective, committed staff you have hired will naturally want you to be involved in all of them. At the beginning of my Senate service, George Mitchell, then majority leader, advised me well to choose three or four areas I wanted to be my priorities. "There are a thousand different issues before the country," he said, "but only a hundred senators, and even fewer Democrats. So the most senior senators can't do it all. If you focus on three or four matters and do your homework, your colleagues will come to rely on you, and you will be able to get a lot done, even as a freshman."

George Mitchell was right, and that's clearly one of the reasons I love the job. I've been able to get some things done. At the beginning, I focused on economic growth, environmental protection and national security. Later, as I watched and learned about the world that my youngest child, Hani, was growing up in, I began to speak out about cultural values, particularly in terms of the powerful entertainment industry. More recently, I have been engaged by the urgent need to reform our education system so that every American child has an equal opportunity to achieve his or her God-given potential.

In each of these areas, I have felt the satisfaction, on a larger stage, that I first felt as a state senator—of taking a principle, an observation or an idea and putting it into a legislative proposal that has made it into law and, therefore, reality.

Lawmaking is a painstaking process in which you have to prepare yourself for incremental progress. My wife says I'm temperamentally suited to be a legislator because I'm patient. It's not a job requirement, but patience helps, so long as it is matched with persistence. Unless you have come up with a new idea that brings change without threatening any established interest, or you are responding to an overwhelming crisis, which all agree requires immediate action, you are very unlikely in Congress to achieve everything you want quickly. That is because we Americans are a diverse people, and every group and idea is represented by an association or a lobbyist in the legislative branch of our democracy. Those associations and lobbyists protect their turf, so to get something done in Congress you have to package your ideas well and market them effectively through the media. You have to gather interest groups to support them, and then convince, cajole and compromise with your colleagues in Congress and the administration to adopt some part of them into law. It is a long road with many turns, but it brings you to progress more often than you expect, and than most people realize.

Although, in the previous chapter, I have lamented the schedule pressures that prevent senators from knowing each other better, it is nevertheless true that in the end the Senate is one hundred people working together. Your ability to get something done often depends on your rapport with your colleagues. A friendly colleague will not help you if you're asking him or her to do something contrary to his or her beliefs or political interests, but that colleague can do a lot if he or she doesn't have a contrary belief or interest in the matter, particularly if you are seeking a program or provision for your home state. Some may find such decision-making and resource allocation to be suspect, but it can produce much good. For example, Connecticut has its first national park site, Weir Farm in Fairfield County, as well as a cleaner Long Island Sound to swim, fish and boat in, and some important urban economic developments because of such collegial courtesies.

Unlike in the House of Representatives, such supportive working relationships among senators often cross party lines.

That's the way it should be, since so many of the issues that come before the Senate are not inherently partisan, and we should not let them artificially become so. For my part, I try never to introduce a major legislative proposal without a Republican co-sponsor if I can find one, and usually I can. I did that when Senate Democrats were in the majority, and, you will not be surprised to learn, I still do it now that the Republicans are in control.

Although special interest groups have contributed greatly to the partisanship and frequent gridlock in Congress, as I will soon explain, they can sometimes help a legislator make the system work. If I can convince an interest group to support one of my legislative proposals, that brings with it lobbying support in Congress and letters and phone calls to every senator from the group's members back home, whether they are environmentalists, municipal officials, realtors, a women's group or any other organized association. That naturally helps broaden the support for my proposal.

At last count, close to 12,000 lobbyists were registered in Washington through the Lobbying Disclosure Act, which became law in 1995. These groups and their particular interests cover the entire political spectrum, from far left to far right. They are not only watching and attempting to influence the members of Congress, but they are also watching one another. One person's bounty is often another person's burden, and in a city like Washington this is particularly true. The result is that everyone on Capitol Hill is keeping a close eye on everyone else, creating a self-adjusting system of checks and balances. The halls of the House and Senate are swarming not only with legislative staff members who comb every bill that comes along, but also with legions of lobbyists doing the same thing. If, for example, some of my colleagues, in the interest of the lumber companies or oil companies in their region, try to put something into an appropriations bill that opens the door to possibly spoiling the environment, the odds are overwhelming that an environmental protection group is going to see that and exert their own pressure to ensure that it doesn't happen.

In the same way that special interest groups have had some positive effects on the Senate, television has also produced some benefit. Rarely does an investigative hearing, the announcement of a legislative proposal or a Senate floor statement occur without some kind of television coverage which, in turn, expands the public's opportunity for access to its government, and for information about what its senators are thinking or doing. Inside the Senate, members appreciate the importance of this coverage and sometimes rank such events by the number of television cameras that attend, as in "I had a five-camera hearing this morning," or "That was a seven-camera press conference." And because this kind of state and national television news coverage of Congress gives members an opportunity to speak over the heads of their party and its leaders to the voters at home, it can facilitate some much-needed nonpartisan independence.

National television news coverage of activities at the Capitol, which has increased significantly in recent years with the arrival of all-news channels, can also make the institution more egalitarian than it used to be. I remember having a conversation a few years ago with a senior Senate colleague about how television has changed Congress, and he said, "In the old days, if I introduced a bill which the chairman of the committee it was referred to didn't like, that was the end of it. I couldn't even get a hearing. Today, if you introduced a bill that I oppose that came to the committee I now chair, and I told you it was dead and I wasn't even going to hold a public hearing on it, the next day you and the groups supporting your bill would go out and hold a press conference on the Capitol steps, and you'd tell all those television cameras how undemocratically I was behaving. And the damn thing is, before the day was out, or the news cycle was over, I would rush to announce the date of a hearing on your bill."

Those are a few of the ways in which special interest groups and television can actually help members of Congress get some things done. Unfortunately, there are many more ways in which they encourage the worst instincts of members and make legislating more difficult.

Not long ago I was at a meeting of the Senate Democrats in which we were discussing the compromises necessary to avoid an impending congressional gridlock with the Republicans over the federal budget. A pollster who had been invited to speak to our group that day rose to explain what he considered an intriguing discovery.

"I know," he told us, "that some of you here feel that there is too much partisanship in Congress, and that when partisanship leads to gridlock, the public is turned off and disgusted by the government in general. And everyone involved suffers politically.

"Well," he continued, "the polling I've done shows something different. According to my findings, it's clear that among people who get angry at government after gridlock occurs, Democrats do much better in the next election."

I could not believe that he was suggesting that it would be advantageous for us as a political party to make sure Congress did nothing, when the country clearly needed us to at least keep the government going. And I was not alone. After a moment or two of silence in the room, one of my colleagues used the word "crazy" to describe what we had just heard.

"Oh, don't get me wrong," the pollster responded. "I'm

not suggesting that you *intentionally* create gridlock. I'm just saying that you don't have to feel that you need to compromise your principles to get something done in a situation like this since it is not going to hurt you politically if you don't."

That scene is typical of what ails our government today. There has always been partisanship in American politics. Historically, much of it has been constructive because the major parties have played a unique and important role by organizing diverse minorities into a coalition to form a majority to govern and make progress. But today, too often, the parties become tactical vehicles for special interests to advance their particular cause or to embarrass the opposition, rather than broadly based coalitions that work together to get something done. The past two decades have seen a sharp rise in enmity between the two major national political parties, and this has severely damaged our perspective and purpose as a united government. The intensity of this "us versus them" mentality has caused a decline in the nobler qualities of political leadership (statesmanship, civility, truthfulness, courage, wisdom, the capacity for compromise) and a rise in the baser aspects of politics (deception, rigidity, meanness, mediocrity, conformity and irrelevance). Winning, which has become the overriding focus of contemporary politics, is not the same as leading, and it is leadership that the American public needs and is asking for in its government today.

I can't speak from personal experience about what the level of partisanship in Washington was like at the time I entered state politics in Connecticut in 1971. But by the time I came to the U.S. Senate in 1989, the lines between the parties had been sharply drawn. When I arrived, it was as if you were on a team, you either wore a blue jersey or a red jersey, and a lot of what you did was expected to be done for your team. There was less actual listening and true exchanging of opposing ideas and opinions between the parties than I had expected. Instead, there was a lot of posturing and confrontation, most of it aimed at establishing or maintaining partisan advantage for the next election. I wasn't new at politics, so I wasn't shocked by this—the rising level of partisanship in Congress in recent years has been no secret. Nonetheless, once I began to experience it firsthand, I was surprised by how deep and pervasive it was.

Even the regular weekly schedule seems to discourage communication and cooperation between the parties. Each Tuesday senators meet separately for lunch in their respective party caucuses. On Wednesdays there are partisan clusters of senators, united by ideology or seniority, that meet separately for lunch. On Thursdays each party has a separate policy lunch. And if a senator gets a chance to go for lunch to the so-called inner sanctum dining room where only senators can go and which is a great place for relaxed conversation, he or she will find two tables, one Republican and one Democratic, each in a separate room.

Many people explain the current hostility between the parties as a clash between cultures, a war between "left" and "right" rooted in the volatile social divisiveness of the 1960s, fomented by the upheaval and aftermath of Watergate in the 1970s, solidified by the Reagan era of the 1980s, and exaggerated by the Republican "revolution" of the 1994 elections and the impeachment of President Clinton in 1998 and 1999. It's true that during this thirty-year period the parties became sharply divided on the issues that mattered most to the American people—crime, welfare, education, taxation, the Cold War, the roles of religion and state. These all became highly partisan issues, and one's views on each of them were largely defined by whether you were "liberal" or "conservative," a Democrat or a Republican. There is some historical truth to this analysis, but, in my opinion, it no longer explains the current partisanship in Congress, nor does it accurately describe the present policy movements of the national political parties.

Most members of the two major political parties *are* in greater ideological agreement with one another than they are with most members of the other party. However, something interesting is happening today in national politics that is diminishing the ideological disagreement. The fact is that the national parties are now moving closer together ideologically, as you can see in the positions taken by their leading presidential candidates this year. This shift can be attributed to what I would call the law of political physics. Parties tend over time to be pulled back toward more moderate positions after they have separated themselves from the majority of Americans by straying to an extreme at either end—left or right—of the political spectrum. Our parties have this natural propensity to return to the center because that's where elections are won in America.

By the mid-1980s, the Democratic Party recognized that it had moved too far to the left in the previous twenty years in several telling ways:

- We seemed to have abandoned the behavioral norms and values of most mainstream Americans in favor of what was perceived by the general public as an "anything goes" mind-set.
- We appeared to defy the fundamental American ethics of work and personal responsibility by creating what seemed to be "free ride" welfare programs at the expense of working people and by appearing to favor the rights of criminals over the rights of victims of crime.

- We cast out religion and faith as having virtually no presence or value whatsoever in politics and public life.
- We seemed to be more concerned with "peace" than with maintaining a necessary level of military strength and national security.

This realization of how far our party had strayed from the heart of America led to the creation in 1985 of the Democratic Leadership Council (DLC), which began framing what has come to be called the New Democratic movement. The DLC was premised on the belief that ideas change history, that elections are about the future and that the Democratic Party had become mired in old ideas that no longer worked. So the DLC began to generate new ideas and programs that applied traditional American values and Democratic principles to current problems and future hopes. The DLC was never an antigovernment movement, but it was always about governmental reform. I followed this exciting new group from its founding in 1985 and became active in it immediately after coming to Washington in 1988. The progress we made in the years that followed was thrilling. In 1992, the DLC's former chairman, Bill Clinton, and its founding member, Al Gore, took the DLC platform and, with it, reconnected with the majority of American voters. After the election, President Clinton and Vice President Gore were able to enact much of the DLC's program, and it has produced a revitalized economy, a governmental surplus, effective welfare reform, lower crime rates and the reintroduction into Democratic national politics of the language and principles of values and religious faith. These were paradigm shifts in our politics as great as the ones President Reagan had brought.

Meanwhile, on the Republican side, the "revolution" that crested in 1994 with the Newt Gingrich–led forces of the right taking control of Congress went too far from mainstream America. What had looked like fiscal responsibility under President Reagan began to seem harsh and mean-spirited under a House Republican–guided party intent on slashing social, educational and environmental programs that many Americans cared about. What had looked like traditional faith and family values under Reagan began to seem like intolerance and intrusiveness as expressed by congressional Republicans. Just as Democrats had strayed too far left of the American center in the 1960s and 1970s, so did the Republicans go too far right in the 1990s. That's one reason the Clinton-Gore administration, solidly in the prosperous and principled center, won a big reelection victory in 1996, and why House Republicans lost seats in 1996 and 1998.

In this year's election, the leading Republican candidate for the presidency, George W. Bush, is obviously trying to bring his party back from the fringe, coining the phrase "compassionate conservatism" as the slogan of his campaign. His use of the word "compassion" is clearly a response to the perceived hard-heartedness of recent Republican leadership, much as our DLC grand trilogy of "opportunity, responsibility and community" was framed to pull our party back from its perceived swing to the anything-goes left. In fact, when Bush ran for reelection as governor of Texas in 1998, he had two words painted on his campaign bus as he rode around the state: "opportunity" and "responsibility." We in the DLC joked that "community" couldn't be far behind. My Senate friend and colleague John McCain of Arizona, who at this writing is seen as the other viable Republican presidential candidate, is also running a certifiably independent and cen-

trist campaign. The laws of political physics are bringing national Republicans back to the center to compete with New
Democrats for the support of the majority of Americans in
this year's presidential election.

Why, then, does there remain so much bitter partisan
combat between the parties in Congress?

One reason is the negative influence of special interest
groups. While the national leadership of each political party
has moved to the middle, there are aggressively activist wings
within each party focused on specific issues or interests—
many of them on a *single* issue—who exercise a much greater
influence than their numbers warrant in each national party
and, in particular, in each party's congressional caucuses. A
survey conducted at the 1996 Republican and Democratic
National Conventions revealed that the delegates chosen for
each of these conventions were not representative of the
rank-and-file membership of the parties. The Republican
delegates were much more conservative than their rank-and-
file colleagues across the country, and the Democratic delegates were much more liberal than the membership they
were chosen to represent. The same is generally true of
members of each party caucus in Congress.

How did this happen? Because the groups in each party
that are at the ideological margins have become very organized and effective in getting their membership actively involved in politics. While the overall number of people who
vote has continued to decline, the number of voters among
these activated interest groups has stayed steady or increased,
so their proportionate influence on the political process has
grown. Not only are these groups not representative of a
broad cross section of America, but they are not even representative of the majority of their own party. Yet, by virtue of

political organization and political contributions, they pull both parties in Congress from the center and agreement toward the margins and gridlock.

The popular public perception that interest groups "buy" the votes of members of Congress is not literally true, but their political contributions certainly do influence the parties. In my own experience I have found it to be not so much individual senators as the national parties and their congressional caucuses that become most dependent on special interest groups for money and grassroots support. They therefore advance the legislative priorities of some of the most ideological of those groups higher on their congressional agenda, which, in turn, further separates the parties and intensifies partisanship.

In this era when television news and paid political commercials so influence public opinion, and so many voters don't even vote anymore, both parties should be skeptical of the promises or threats of special interest groups to "deliver" voters to the polls. But campaign contributions are tangible and quantifiable, and since they are what get candidates and parties on television, which does deliver voters, a special interest group's ability to raise money definitely can move the parties in Congress—which is to say, pull them further apart ideologically and politically.

When it comes to individual members of Congress, the interest groups understand that what money *can* buy is access. Certainly they want your vote on issues of concern to them, but they realize that the first step to gaining your support is getting your ear, or your staff's ear. They need just a little time in a very busy day, when you or your staff can't see everyone who wants to see you.

Part of an elected official's responsibility, part of his obligation, is to lend that ear and to give that time. I have always felt that if somebody or some group has supported me, I owe them a hearing, or at the very least a hearing with a member of my staff. Please understand that I am speaking here of the widest range of interest groups—from investment bankers and doctors who do give contributions, to senior citizens and environmentalists who generally don't but can influence votes. When it comes to votes in the Senate, I first consider the merits of the issue. If I have a strong opinion about the issue, I am going to vote that way, regardless of the preferences of any interest group or even of the general public, as I will explain in a moment. If I do not have a strong opinion one way or the other on a particular issue—if I don't see a clear right and wrong way to go—then I'll probably go ahead and try to help out a group that has supported me, particularly if that group is from Connecticut—with one big exception. If I conclude that a majority of my constituents have a strong opinion on an issue, and I do not, then I will vote my constituents' opinion regardless of what the special interests want. That is true of most members of Congress and, of course, is the way our democracy is supposed to work.

After a couple of years in the Senate, I became troubled by the fact that almost all of the people asking to talk with me in my Hartford and Washington offices were representatives of organized interest groups. The same was true of most of the people who turned out at the open town hall meetings I was holding. These interest groups have a right to speak to their senator and I have a responsibility to listen to them, but that wasn't enough. I wanted to hear the views of the average, unorganized people in the state, the silent majority. I decided to visit diners and luncheonettes and go from table to table with a tuna sandwich and a cup of coffee, asking the people there either what they thought of a particular debate then going on in Washington or if they had any message they would like their senator to bring back to the Capitol. Visiting almost one hundred and fifty diners all over the state during the last ten years, I have learned a lot from the people there that has helped me better represent their views in Washington. In fact, there have been many times when someone at a diner has said something to me that has led to a hearing or the introduction of legislation.

Once, after I voted against a pay raise for senators, my highly disappointed wife said, "If you guys will vote against something like that which is in the clear interest of your families just because it is unpopular with the voters, I don't see why any interest group would ever have any confidence you would stick with them." She had a good point.

In politics there is no such thing as total independence. You are, by the nature of the process, bound to the people who elect you, to the people who support you politically and financially, to the people who work with and for you during your campaigns and during your time in office, and to the American people as a whole. With that understood, it is not only possible, but beneficial, for a public servant to establish, develop and maintain a good measure of independence, and to be true to his or her conscience.

Although both parties and many politicians act as if they believe the partisan strategies they follow will make them more popular and help them win elections, they are wrong. Most of the voters are fed up and turned off by all the partisanship. They want their elected officials to be as independent as they are, to be individuals instead of members of a herd. Very few voters support a proposal just because it is advanced by their party. They support it because they think it is sensible or right, and that's exactly what they want their elected representatives to do. So, while political independence does not usually please the inner elite of partisan activists and can affect your ability to influence your party, it is likely to earn a politician support among the voters at large.

Back when I was a senior at college, working on my thesis about John Bailey, I interviewed a businessman from Westport, Connecticut, Jerry Kaiser (his nephew is Bob Kaiser, my college classmate, who went on to become managing editor of the *Washington Post*). During the course of that interview Kaiser, who was involved in state Democratic politics, said something I have never forgotten. "Kid," he told me, "here's a lesson I'll give you for going into politics. You cannot do everything you need to do by yourself. You're always going to have to be dependent on people, so what you've got to do is spread your dependencies around, so *you* can be independent."

During my entire career, I have tried to follow Kaiser's counsel and not become overly dependent on any group or individual. When it comes to campaign contributions, the post-Watergate reforms actually made that easier because they prohibit me or any other candidate for Congress or president from accepting more than $2,000 from any individual or $10,000 from any PAC in an election cycle. So if it costs almost $6 million to run for the Senate in Connecticut, and an individual who gave me the maximum $2,000 or a PAC that gave me $10,000 then comes and asks me to cast a vote that I don't think is right, or that I believe a majority of my constituents will not view as correct, then I will listen to them but I will ultimately not be pressured to vote with them. Human and political natures being what they are, I cannot honestly say that members of Congress would feel similarly unpressured if that individual or PAC group could, for example, give a campaign $100,000 or $500,000 or more.

The existence of such big money pressure—or even the

appearance of it—has done terrible damage to the public's trust in their government and has created profound cynicism about our political system's promise that every citizen has equal access to our government. That was painfully demonstrated during the Senate's 1997 investigation into campaign finance abuses.

Those hearings focused on the "soft money" loophole that allows individuals and groups to give $100,000 or $500,000 or more, particularly to presidential candidates. I was a member of the committee conducting that investigation and listened with revulsion to dozens of witnesses as they described the rampant influence-peddling that occurred during those elections. Some of these individuals were brazen beyond the point of belief, such as businessman Roger Tamraz, an international financier whose background was, to say the least, shadowy (the Interpol had an arrest warrant out for him in connection with embezzlement charges in Lebanon). Tamraz wanted to build an oil pipeline in the Caspian Sea area and tried to convince our government to help his project. After he was turned down by the National Security Council, Tamraz contributed more than $300,000 to various Democratic committees and candidates and attended several events at which President Clinton was present and where Tamraz tried to personally make his case to the President. In this case the access didn't help. Even though high-level Democratic officials looked into the matter again on Tamraz's behalf, his efforts were ultimately unsuccessful. I asked him about that during the hearings.

"So," I said, "do you think you got your money's worth? Do you feel badly about having given the three hundred thousand dollars?"

He didn't blink.

"I think," he answered, "next time I'll give six hundred thousand."

This, from an American citizen who, when I later asked when and where he was registered to vote, breezily acknowledged that he had never bothered to register to vote. He didn't have to. Big-money contributions got him much, much more than a vote would have, the vote that generations of Americans have fought and died for. Is it any wonder that the average American citizen, after witnessing such shameless bartering of access and influence among both major parties, would feel that our politicians have, as my report on the investigation concluded, "effectively hung out a giant 'For Sale' sign on our government and the whole of our political process"?

American politicians have become so hungry for campaign contributions largely because, as I noted earlier, so much of politics has become driven by and wedded to television, which costs a lot of money. In 1994, which was a midterm election year, a record-shattering total of $356 million was spent by the nation's political candidates (at local, state and national levels) on TV ads. That figure was unimaginable just a decade earlier. Two years later, with the presidency on the line, that number jumped to $405 million. The most recent midterm elections, in 1998, saw an astounding $532 million poured into television by political campaigns. At that rate, by the time the ongoing presidential-year election races are decided this November, a total of roughly $700 million will have been paid to the television advertising industry by the men and women running for public office in America.

Too much of those millions is raised today by both the Democratic and Republican Parties in the form of soft money, with much of it spent on television advertisements that skirt regulations on political spending by promoting or attacking a particular candidate without using words like "vote for" or "vote against."

In the wake of the 1997 campaign finance investigation, I hoped that the American people would rise up and demand reform from Congress, but there was instead an eerie public silence. There were editorials, of course, and the pleas of a few advocacy groups, but the general public was either distracted or resigned. Part of this was due to the eruption of the Lewinsky scandal, which captured the media spotlight at the same time we could have been passing campaign finance reform. But part was also due, I'm afraid, to a sense of fatalism on the part of the American people concerning their government and politics. A Gallup survey done in 1997, after our investigation, revealed that nearly 60 percent of Americans believe that America's elections are essentially on the auction block and feel that a campaign finance reform bill would be futile since special interests will always find a way to maintain power in Washington, regardless of the laws that are passed. When the majority of Americans feel this way, a cycle of cynicism is created that perpetuates itself and drags our democracy down.

It will take a lot of courage and independence by elected officials to break this cycle and regain the public's trust. And that will not be easy in the present political environment of "permanent campaigning." When the governmental process is working well, it is one of discussion, accommodation and solutions. It is about exploring problems and opportunities, creating coalitions and getting things done. That is good government. Political campaigning is something altogether different. While legislating is—or should be—constructive and additive, campaigning is zero-sum and destructive, in the sense that you aim to defeat your opponent. In the legislature, both sides can win. In a campaign, only one side wins.

The problem in Congress today is that campaigns never end. Legislating has become campaigning by another name, which often means not much legislating gets done. Elected officials at the federal level regularly position themselves for the next campaign. They focus too much on raising the vast sums of money needed for expensive television advertising, and worry too often about the ramifications of a single vote they cast, for fear that it may come back to haunt them on television in the next election.

At a time when we need more courage and independence among our elected leaders, this last point is critical because of the timidity it creates. In the past, an elected official was usually confident his career would not ride on one legislative vote. If a politician took an unpopular stand on a particular issue, the newspapers would cover it and his opponent might raise it in speeches, but on balance, come election time, it would be considered in the context of his overall stance on the broad range of issues he faced during his entire term in office and on what he had done for his constituents. A U.S. senator today casts about 350 votes a year. That adds up to roughly 2,100 votes during a six-year term. In the past, that senator would usually be judged, come election time, on the overall record of those 2,100 votes, as well as his constituent service. Today, however, a single vote can kill you because it can become the subject of an attack television commercial at the end of your next campaign. The meaning of any single vote can be immensely magnified and manipulated by a legislator's political or ideological opponents.

Accountability is a good thing, of course. But this quantum leap in pinpoint exposure can create hypersensitivity among legislators that makes it harder for them to find either the courage to be independent or the capacity to compromise that are required for truly effective government. It fosters caution rather than boldness and can create legislators who are tempted before casting a controversial vote to first put their finger to the wind, perhaps even conducting an overnight poll or surveying a staff of hired consultants. These tools—polls, consultants, the modern technology available for instant gathering and dissemination of information—can be very helpful, but they must be used with the understanding that they have limits, that they are, in the end, still *tools*. We wield them, and we must control them. When we as legislators allow them to control us, the result is "followership" rather than leadership.

When I arrived in Washington in 1989, I felt that I had achieved my dream, that by the grace of God and the support of the voters of Connecticut, I had become a United States senator. In my career, I wanted nothing more. My mission, as I saw it, was to try to make a difference by doing what I thought was right and to trust that the people who elected me would want it that way. Even though the scope and the stakes were larger than when I arrived in Hartford at the Connecticut state senate eighteen years before, I was much more confident. Back then, if I received five or ten letters or calls from constituents who felt differently about a matter than I did, I would become very anxious about how to vote— even though my district had 70,000 residents. With time and experience, I came to understand that people—not all the people, but certainly most of them—want you to do what you think is right, even if they disagree with you. In other words, the fear I have talked about, that a lot of elected officials have today that one attack television advertisement about one vote will bring them down in the next election, is unwarranted. The voters are usually fair. They *will* judge you on your entire record and your sincerity.

My own capacity for legislative and political independence was strengthened by the political traditions of Connecticut, which have always encouraged and rewarded independence, and by the particular circumstances of my 1988 Senate election. Remember, I received an unusual group of Republican endorsements and the votes of a lot of Republicans. So, from the beginning, though I was a committed New Democrat, I felt a special responsibility to listen to and represent the views of Republicans and independents as well.

All this helped me focus on my goal of making a difference. If making that difference meant crossing party lines to work and to vote for values and programs I believe in, so be it. I have faced situations in the Senate that have put me at odds with most members of my own party—for example, voting in favor of the Gulf war, supporting a capital gains tax cut and, yes, publicly criticizing the leader of my own party. Some of these decisions were highly unpopular with a significant number of Democrats at the time they were made. But with time, and on balance, I think most people have either agreed with those decisions or respected them even if they disagreed. Clearly, many others have not, but if you want everybody to agree with you, you should choose a career other than politics.

You don't have to be a political scientist or a consultant speaking to a caucus to know that the public prefers progress to stalemate and will favor elected officials in both parties who cooperate to produce results. In fact, even during the largely partisan time I have been in the Senate, there have been some major accomplishments that resulted from bipartisan cooperation: the Clean Air Act of 1990, the NAFTA and GATT trade agreements of 1993, the anti-crime law of

1994, the ISTEA transportation reforms of 1994, the welfare reforms of 1996 and the Balanced Budget Agreement of 1997. These were historic achievements and proved that in spite of the partisanship, the negative influence of special interest groups and the corrosiveness of big money in campaigns, Congress is able, with the right leadership and the appropriate accommodations to one another, to make a difference for the public good.

There are many men and women of integrity, courage and wise practicality who serve in Congress today, although they are too often overshadowed by the partisan crossfire. But, believe me, they are here and they make the place produce when it does. And even when it doesn't, they can act in a principled way that makes me proud to serve with them and should make their constituents proud to be represented by them. These colleagues have taught me a lot about lawmaking and helped me get some good things done in Congress. Now, I want to mention a few of the legislative success stories I have been privileged to be involved in so you will understand why I am so glad I decided more than thirty-five years ago to go into politics, and why I write now in praise of public life.

NATIONAL SECURITY: When Saddam Hussein's Iraqi forces invaded Kuwait in 1990, I felt America's post–Cold War commitment to national principles and international leadership was on the line. After President Bush ordered half a million American soldiers to the region, I was dismayed by the wide opposition among my fellow Democrats. To me, their position was wrong if they had reached it on policy grounds, and terribly wrong if they were simply trying to gain partisan advantage.

That December, George Mitchell invited Senate Democrats to lunch in groups of ten or so to ask a preliminary question: Did we feel that President Bush should come to Congress for authorization before launching a war against Iraq? I couldn't stay until the end of the meeting, so I got up and said, "I definitely think the President should come to Congress for authorization, but I want you to know that if he does, I will support him." Everyone in the room was silent and seemed surprised.

In January, because I was one of the few Democrats publicly supporting Bush's policy, Deputy Secretary of State Lawrence Eagleburger called and asked if I would be the lead Democratic co-sponsor (with Republican John Warner of Virginia) of the Senate resolution authorizing the President to take military action in Iraq. After a lot of work, the resolution passed, by a slim margin of 52–47, with ten Democrats supporting it. I remember telling Hadassah when I came home that night that if I did nothing else of value in my Senate career, co-sponsoring and working for the votes to pass that Gulf war resolution would make it worthwhile.

Late in 1991, a different kind of challenge to America's principles and international leadership occurred when Serb forces under Slobodan Milosevic went from attacking Slovenia and Croatia to slaughtering Bosnians. The more I learned about what was happening in the Balkans, the stronger I felt that we had to intervene, to stop a wider war in Europe and prevent another genocide there. The administration and most of my colleagues in Congress were hesitant, but Bob Dole, a hero of World War II and exemplar of "The Greatest Generation," was not. He and I formed an alliance and adopted a legislative strategy. We would counter the haze of arguments about why we should not or could not stop the bloodshed in Bosnia with a proposal to lift the embargo on arms sales so that the Bosnians could at least defend themselves. We offered the proposal for a vote three times over the next three years, pushing our colleagues to think hard about the implications of their votes. Each time we gained more support because of the spreading awareness of the tragedy that was unfolding. Finally, in the spring of 1995, after a massacre in Bosnia at Srebenica, our resolution passed. A Senate majority had voted for intervention. Together with the rising public revulsion with Srebenica, the Senate vote helped move the administration to convince NATO to bomb Serb targets, which in turn led to the peace conference at Dayton, Ohio, the end of the Bosnian war, and renewed respect for the U.S. and NATO.

Our experience in Bosnia brought about quicker and more extensive NATO military intervention to stop the next European aggression, in Kosovo, and, in a different way, encouraged us to support UN action to end the human rights outrages in East Timor, both of which I supported.

DEFENSE REFORM: Like so many Americans, I have always held Winston Churchill up as a hero for his leadership during the Second World War and before. Earlier in my life, I had read just about everything there is to read about Churchill's crusade to rebuild Britain's military between the wars. That all came back to me after our Cold War victory over the Soviet Union and Communism, when we began to cut military spending. We seemed invulnerable, even though we faced new responsibilities like international peacekeeping and new threats from terrorism and ballistic missiles with chemical, biological or nuclear warheads. I worried that America was lowering its guard. Encouraged by Sam Nunn of Georgia, another one of my Senate mentors, I joined the Armed Services Committee and began to argue for more money for the military and for different ways of spending it that would anticipate and prepare us for the next century's threats to America's security.

With Republicans Dan Coats of Indiana and John McCain of Arizona, and Democrat Chuck Robb of Virginia, I introduced legislation in 1996 to require the Pentagon and a team of outside experts to look beyond the near-time horizon, ten or twenty years into the future, to estimate what international dangers the U.S. might have to deal with and come back and tell us what we should be investing in now to be sure we will be ready then. The legislation passed and resulted in some bold proposals for a transformational approach to military preparedness, pulling away from the so-called legacy weapons systems of the Cold War and investing in the research and development that would produce higher-tech weapons for the next generations.

I then drafted and secured passage of legislation to implement parts of this transformational strategy. First, Dan Coats and I offered a proposal to break the redundant and wasteful separate service (Army, Navy, Air Force and Marines) approach to weapons requirements, experimentation and war-fighting. It resulted in the assignment of special responsibilities for developing more "joint experimentation" among the services to the Atlantic Command (now known as the Joint Forces Command) in Norfolk, Virginia, along with some money which has already helped to make more joint activity occur in the Pentagon.

Last year, after Coats's retirement, I worked with Republican senators Pat Roberts of Kansas and Rick Santorum of Pennsylvania and Democrat Jeff Bingaman of New Mexico to propose and pass legislation that will restructure and reform the Pentagon's research and development operations. This new law will create more pressure inside the military to stay on the cutting edge of innovation, and offers incentives to defense companies to make it more profitable for them to innovate rather than to keep producing systems that make money for their companies (because the Pentagon keeps buying them) but are no longer needed, at least in such quantities, by our military.

Unlike some of the other "success stories" in my Senate career, these defense reforms receive very little media attention outside the trade press and we have to continually work with the bureaucracy on implementation. But I am convinced they represent one of the greatest contributions I can make to my country.

ECONOMIC GROWTH: We New Democrats believe that the booming economy of the 1990s resulted more from private sector innovation, investment and hard work than from government actions, but the federal government sure can and did help. The Clinton-Gore administration deserves tremendous credit for their leadership in the 1993 balanced budget proposal, and the NAFTA and GATT trade agreements that followed, which showed that they were committed to fiscal responsibility and global competitiveness. Both were controversial and difficult to pass. The 1993 budget did not receive a single Republican vote in either chamber, while the trade agreements split congressional Democrats down the middle. I am proud that I stood with the President and Vice President on both of these policies, and believe strongly that they shaped the economic environment in which we have enjoyed such unprecedented growth.

Because I have always believed that tax policy can influence economic behavior and I was troubled by the lack of capital investment in our economy during the late 1980s and early 1990s, I supported a cut in the capital gains tax. In 1989, I was one of six Democrats to vote for President Bush's capital gains tax proposal. Later I joined Orrin Hatch, Republican senator from Utah, to co-sponsor the capital gains tax cut which finally passed in 1997. I believe the record shows it has helped to keep the American economy growing.

The booming economy has raised many millions of people with it, but left millions of others behind. Our government can and should do something about that. During my first year in the Senate, influenced by good experience with enterprise zones in Connecticut and some excellent research and advocacy by the Heritage Foundation in Washington, I joined with Jack Kemp, then at HUD, and Democrat Charlie Rangel of New York to introduce legislation that offered tax incentives, grants and regulatory relief to woo businesses and jobs into our poorest urban and rural areas. President Clinton embraced the idea and it was finally adopted in 1997. It is starting to work to spread opportunity and wealth.

In 1998, I supported a proposal to raise the annual limit on five-year visas for skilled workers from foreign countries to fill high-tech jobs for which employers could not find enough American employees. When opposition emerged from some labor unions and others, I took a bright idea that had been produced by the Progressive Policy Institute of the DLC to create regional skills alliances of businesses, community colleges and government to train American workers to fill job shortages and, along with Democrat Paul Sarbanes of Maryland, turned it into an amendment to the visa bill. Our proposal also directed that the fee for the visas be increased and the money be used to fund the government's share of the skills alliances. My Republican partner in this was Spencer Abraham of Michigan, who had sponsored the visa increase. It was one of those rare cases where a new idea emerges which responds to a real problem and threatens no established interest, so it passed quickly and unanimously. Now we are battling the bureaucracy to implement it.

ENVIRONMENT: The Clean Air Act of 1990 was my first involvement in a successful marathon effort to pass important legislation. As a member of the Senate Environment Committee, I had a seat at the table in the small, crowded conference room adjoining Majority Leader George Mitchell's office, where Mitchell adeptly presided over weeks of daily negotiations with the Bush administration and senators representing a difficult and dizzying array of regional or state environmental and industrial interests. The bipartisan result was a law which has cleaned our air and improved our health. Because I was there, I was able to achieve some very good results, particularly protecting Connecticut and other states in the Northeast from acid rain and air pollution blowing in from the midwest and the south.

Some of the most satisfying work I have done in the Senate has turned out to be in open space and natural resource conservation. We saved Weir Farm in Wilton and Ridgefield, a beautiful center of American impressionist painting, as Connecticut's first national park site, and created a Long Island Sound office to oversee the cleanup of that great body of water, along with a Connecticut River fish and wildlife refuge to preserve the gains we have made in purifying and protecting what Connecticut's own Katharine Hepburn once called "America's best landscaped cesspool."

These legislative accomplishments give me such satisfaction because they are tangible and visible and because the protection of land and nature that they accomplish will be long-lasting, perhaps even permanent.

CULTURAL VALUES: Watching my youngest daughter watch television as it became more coarsely sexual and violent is what moved me first to speak out about the harmful impact of so much of the entertainment industry's products on our culture and on our children. Because of my devotion to the First Amendment, most of my work here has amounted to advocacy with my friend Bill Bennett, not with my legislative colleagues. Herb Kohl of Wisconsin and I did propose a government board to develop a rating system for video games which, as we had hoped, induced the industry to produce one of its own. It turned out to be the clearest and most informational of any media rating system. Then, in 1995, Kent Conrad of North Dakota and I decided to take Congressman Ed Markey's proposal for an electronic blocking device, the now famous V-chip, to empower parents to screen out undesired shows or channels and introduce it as an amendment to a major telecommunications bill that was then on the Senate floor. The broadcast industry was enthusiastically for the underlying bill but against our amendment, which they had not expected. They lobbied hurriedly and hard against us, as did the Senate's leaders. But by then the public was fed up with much of television and their senators knew it. When the roll was called, the vote was close. As we approached and then achieved a majority, the stunned Senate leadership began to try to change votes, keeping the roll open much longer than the prescribed twenty minutes. When our support held at fifty votes and the opposition gave up, there was a surge of senators to change their recorded votes. I remember Al D'Amato asking the chair, "Mr. President, how am I recorded?" and the presiding officer answering with uncommon directness, "The senator from New York is recorded on the wrong side." We ended up after all the vote-switching with seventy-three votes, and television ultimately got a rating system and electronic blocker which, though far from perfect, are there to help parents protect their kids from the worst of television, if they want to.

Beyond my work on the floor of the Senate, there is a side of the senatorial life which rarely receives public notice but is critical to the lives of the people involved and often gives me more satisfaction than anything I do in Washington. I'm talking about the numerous individual cases of appeals for assistance or justice that are brought to my state office by people who live in Connecticut:

> • People like Rudy Raffone of East Haven, a World War II Army vet who was wounded in Normandy and received battlefield treatment that included a blood transfusion. That transfusion led to hepatitis C, which lay dormant in Rudy's body for the next forty-five years. He didn't discover it until he was diagnosed with liver cancer in the late 1980s. Just before Rudy died, in 1992, Ken Dagliere of my Hartford staff helped him file a service-connected disability claim with the Veterans Administration. Following his death, the VA denied the claim, and my office appealed the decision. Five years after that, in 1997, the Board of Veteran Appeals in D.C. reversed the decision and awarded a retroactive check of $37,000 to Rudy's widow, Anne, along with a monthly benefit of $831 for life. Sadly, Mrs. Raffone passed away less than a year after that, but because of her husband's case, the VA changed its policy toward consideration of hepatitis C's link to liver cancer and other fatal illnesses, and sent out letters nationwide to vets who had had

such claims denied, informing them that their cases would be reviewed.

• Then there was the case of Frank and Nga Jaworski of Stamford, who met and married while Frank was serving in the Vietnam War and returned to the United States in 1969 to start a family. After the South Vietnamese government collapsed in 1975, three of Nga's four sisters, along with her half sister, managed to escape Vietnam and emigrate to the United States, where they joined Frank and Nga in Stamford. However, Nga's remaining sister, Pham, did not make it out. Trapped by the new Vietnamese government's procedures and an unimaginably long waiting list for petitions to emigrate to the United States, Pham waited seventeen years while her petition inched up the list. In 1992, Pham died from colon cancer related to wartime spraying of her village with Agent Orange. The day after her death, the immigrant visas she had applied for arrived at her home, but when her children, Thao and Hieu, presented their new visas, they were revoked by the Immigration and Naturalization Service because their mother had died. The children's situation was dire; their father was in jail, his relatives refused to care for either child, and their mother's family were all in the United States.

After Frank and Nga contacted my Hartford office in 1995, Laura Cahill of my staff filed a humanitarian parole request with the INS, which was denied. Laura and I were so moved by the plight of these two Vietnamese children that I did something I had never done before. I called INS Commissioner Doris Meissner and pleaded with her to overrule the denial. In January 1996 she did exactly that, approving both children for visas. That September, Thao and Hieu came to the United States and were reunited with Frank, Nga and their entire extended Vietnamese family. I felt as if we had helped save their lives.

Every senator and congressman in Washington can cite hundreds of cases like these in his or her home state or district. They mean so much to us because each case is so personal and so real. It is casework victories like these and legislative successes like the ones described earlier that have ultimately made my job so satisfying. They also explain why I recommend public service and public life to anyone, young or old, who wants to make a difference.

9

THE FUTURE

MUCH HAS BEEN MADE of the fact that virtually every candidate for president in the 2000 election has put religion at the center of his or her campaign. The candidates have openly discussed their personal faith and proposed government support of faith-based organizations as an effective way to treat many social ills. Cynics dismiss this as a purely political response to polls that show most Americans are more concerned right now about the moral health of our society than about even their economic well-being. But I think there is much more to this turn toward faith among presidential candidates than political strategy. I see it as a sincere reflection of the need the American people have to rebuild around themselves what has come to feel like a crumbling moral framework in the life of our nation.

Our society has been shaken by a succession of morally jolting events during the past several years. There was, of course, the Clinton-Lewinsky scandal and the impeachment trauma that followed it. There was the horrific tragedy at Littleton, Colorado, along with similar acts of violence among schoolchildren and in workplaces elsewhere across the nation. There has been a disturbing rise in violent hate crimes and unprecedented terrorist attacks by some Americans against their own government and their fellow citizens. And there is a swelling sense that much of our culture has become toxic, that our standards of decency and civility are being significantly eroded by the entertainment industry's shameless and pervasive promotion of violence, sex and vulgarity, and that the traditional sources of values in our society—such as faith, family and school—are in a life and death struggle with the darker forces of immorality, inhumanity and greed.

This series of shocks to our collective consciousness has accelerated an ongoing national dialogue about our priorities, values and standards. We have come to one of those points, which arise in the course of a democratic society's history, where we feel a need to define and clarify who we are, what we believe in and what we expect from one another. More and more of us are engaged in a moral reexamination of ourselves, our families, our communities, our society and our elected leaders—their duties and behavior, public and private. This is ultimately a very personal process in which we are increasingly turning to each other for help. I will never forget the woman who stopped me at a supermarket in New Haven and pleaded with me to continue my efforts to clean up the entertainment culture. "I feel as if I'm in a competition with television and movies and music to raise my own children and give them good values," she said. "Sometimes I think about calling the local television station or writing to Hollywood. But they won't listen to me. Maybe they will listen to you, Senator."

Beginning with the founders of our country and the framers of its Constitution, each succeeding generation of Americans that has faced such a time of crisis has turned to God and to America's civil religion for strength and purpose. We are, after all, not just a nation. We are, as our Pledge of Allegiance declares, "one nation, under God." So it is not surprising that in the current time of crisis, we are again turning to faith and experiencing what may be a spiritual awakening that can lead to social and political renewal. Nor is it surprising in this democracy of ours that political candidates, including those running for president this year, are sincerely reflecting that return to faith in their lives and in their campaigns.

The first great awakening, which occurred in colonial America during the eighteenth century, helped lead to the liberation of churches from state control and energized the movement for independence from England, and freedom. The second great awakening happened in the first half of the nineteenth century and spawned the view that just as individuals could achieve redemption, so too could the country be redeemed by the work of social improvement. Evangelicals of that day helped found the abolitionist movement, which led the way eventually to the end of slavery.

I am going to argue here that there are clear signs of the beginning of a new American awakening around our country today, and that it desperately requires more Americans to become active in public life before it can bring about the political and cultural redemption America needs. Today's awakening is appropriately multi-denominational and broadly spiritual. From it, our country now needs a political awakening to restore our government's clarity of purpose, its integrity of action and its credibility among the American people. I want to begin by discussing the broader cultural decline we have experienced, and then describe how I believe it has coincided with and contributed to our governmental decline, and finally explain why I am hopeful about the future.

This nation was built on a foundation of values—of individual rights and freedoms, of equal opportunity and tolerance. These are values we treasure, and well we should. They are fundamental to the American experience and identity. But this nation was also built on the rule of law, codes of behavior enacted by the people's representatives to protect individual freedom and also to protect each of us from the others by imposing community standards. Unlimited freedom would lead to chaos. Where we draw the lines between liberty and limits, between the freedom of the individual and the values of the community, is a recurring question in a free society like ours. It is a critical question at this moment, when so many Americans have lost faith in the integrity of their government and its leaders—respectively, the very institution and individuals we have typically turned toward to help us draw those lines.

What makes this a particularly perplexing time is that the crisis we face now is not rooted in the economy, or education, or the environment, or crime, or civil and human rights, or health care, or national defense, or international relations, or any of the myriad issues with which the American people and their government leaders typically grapple, although it touches many of those concerns. This one is rooted in our *selves,* our values and the broad cultural and moral environment in which we are living our lives and raising our children.

That word itself—"values"—has become a weapon in the partisan conflicts that have divided our politics and our culture over the last thirty years. When the left heard the right use the term "values," they heard it as a code word for intolerance, censorship, intrusive government and the loss of personal freedoms. When the right heard the left use the word "values," they heard it as a synonym for "anything goes," an open door that allows and excuses any behavior, with little or no regard for its moral content or consequences in the community; they saw it as an invitation to the break-

down of authority and the loss of accountability that under-
mine many of our basic institutions today.

The majority of Americans belong to neither ideological camp and have been either confused or repelled by this
values debate. Faced with a choice some found uncomfortable and others found unrealistic, the majority have remained silent and thereby left the public definition of our
values to the partisan combatants in the culture wars. As a result, we have lost our *public* consensus about values. We have
also lost sight of something that is critically important. Our
personal values do *not* actually divide us as much as the public torchbearers of left and right and the news media who
often fan their flames would have us believe. The fact is that
the majority of Americans continue to stand on common
moral ground. We agree upon and share the same core values that have guided us through our entire history—the fundamental principles and moral assumptions that unite us as
Americans and that have served as the foundation of our
democracy since its inception. These core values, expressed
in the common principles of our major religions, are in the
Declaration of Independence, the Constitution and the Bill
of Rights. They include respect for the dignity of each
human life, individual freedom, equal opportunity, tolerance,
self-government, limited government, personal and civic responsibility, and a belief in the existence of higher laws of
right and wrong that unites us as a people.

An important study was published in 1998 by the
Boston University sociologist Alan Wolfe that validates pre-
cisely this point. Based on interviews with two hundred mid-
dle-class Americans in eight different communities across
the country, Dr. Wolfe set out to see if a deep divide over
cultural and moral values actually exists among mainstream
Americans. His results, published in a book aptly titled *One*

Nation, After All, show, to the surprise of many, that there is an extraordinarily high degree of agreement across ideological, theological, racial and ethnic lines on the core set of common values—a level of agreement that bridges all our many differences as Americans. That agreement, in turn, helps explain why the law of political physics I described in the previous chapter eventually brings political parties and candidates back to the middle, which is also the common ground of shared values.

But Dr. Wolfe also found a correspondingly high degree of reluctance on the part of the men and women he surveyed to translate their privately held values into public expressions that hold others accountable to those shared standards. The common refrain Dr. Wolfe heard was that people did not want to appear intolerant and did not feel comfortable "imposing" their morality on their neighbors or fellow citizens. That is a relatively recent phenomenon in American life.

There is absolutely no question that our society's increase in tolerance over the course of the past half century has made us a much better country, truer to our founding ideals of equality and opportunity than we ever were before. We have opened a new world of more equal opportunities to women while still working to eradicate continuing biases against them. We have made great progress over the last generation in fighting bigotry and discrimination against African-Americans and other racial and ethnic minorities, making more real for them, after a terrible history of inequity and injustice, the equality of opportunity promised by the Declaration of Independence. And we have more recently begun to confront and eliminate bias and discrimination against homosexuals.

But in our worthy, even noble pursuit of these changes, we appear to have become so wary of being labeled intolerant that we were increasingly unwilling to assert long-held communal values and make moral judgments. We confused tolerance and respect for all people with tolerance and acceptance of all behavior. We forgot that some behaviors are simply intolerable. This moral timidity in the name of tolerance deprived us of the common vocabulary of values and the shared moral assumptions that traditionally have been at the heart of the American experience and that any society needs to maintain its well-being and inform its public policies and laws. From the 1960s to the 1980s, the interests of the individual took such broad precedence over the desires of the community and its values that public morality in America suffered a very damaging decline.

That is evident in our families, where we have gone from completely stigmatizing divorce and out-of-wedlock childbirth to normalizing those choices so that there is much too little concern for the damage they do to children individually and to society as a whole.

It is also evident in our schools, where too many teachers and curricula have avoided mentioning the words "values" and "faith," and have refused to help children understand the difference between right and wrong for fear of causing controversy, offending someone or inviting a lawsuit.

It is true in our public ceremonies and places where courts and officials have repeatedly prohibited expressions of faith, thus mistaking the Constitution's promise of freedom of religion for a policy of freedom from religion. That has deprived America of one of its greatest sources of strength, unity and guidance.

It is particularly harmful in the entertainment industry, where executives of multi-billion-dollar conglomerates use the First Amendment as a constitutional hall pass that allows them to produce and market music centered on cop-killing, gang rape and the sexualization of children; video games that reward players for graphically splattering human targets with semiautomatic weapons and homicidal hot rods; motion pictures and television programs that present sex as a casual recreational pastime and violence as a thrilling sport; and television talk shows that degrade the human spirit by revelling in the exploitation of human misery and perversity.

I am absolutely convinced that a connection exists between our reluctance to express and enforce commonly held moral standards and the increase of social pathologies around us: the disintegration of too many of our communities and families; the general coarsening of conversations and communications in our shared public spaces; the ongoing epidemics of children giving birth to children and of sexually transmitted diseases among teenagers; and the sense of isolation, emptiness and nihilism that has led a disturbing number of children and adults to lash out in horrific explosions of frustrated, aimless savagery.

People need expectations and standards, lines drawn around us that define who we are and make us a community. We need to remember that the Declaration of Independence is also a declaration of *inter*dependence. The values declared in that document and in the Constitution and the Bill of Rights make us into a community. They express our shared sense of right and wrong, our common destiny. When we allow this sense to diminish, our feeling of connection to one another—as families, as communities, as a country—diminishes as well.

While the majority of Americans continue, within their own lives and families, to maintain a state of moral equilibrium (a healthy balance between freedom, tolerance and standards), a state of moral *dis*equilibrium (in which, as the

Reverend Billy Graham has put it, "liberty has become confused with license") has crept into and infected some of our
most important and powerful institutions, including the entertainment industry, the news media and, most pointedly
(and disappointingly), our government.

To me, the troubles within each of these three institutions now seem connected, as if a virus had spread among already ailing bodies to make the health of each worse. The
moral disequilibrium of the entertainment industry has infected the news media, which, in turn, has further endangered the health of our government.

The entertainment industry is just that, an industry—a
big industry—and, as such, its executives face the same pressures to increase quarterly profits as the leaders of any other
business do. Too often in recent years, they have responded
to that pressure by producing television shows, movies,
music and video games that reach for the lowest common de-
nominator of sex, violence and vulgarity. This is often an act
of executive cautiousness because you can usually attract an
audience by appealing to the lesser inclinations of people:
remember, the Romans regularly filled the Coliseum to see
Christians fed to the lions. It is at the same time an act of
corporate irresponsibility because the consequences of these
business decisions are very harmful to our children and, in
fact, to adults. The resulting entertainment culture shapes
values and influences behavior. It does not, as the industry
often argues, merely reflect societal norms. It also affects
public standards and taste, including what people look for in
the news media, and how news editors and producers respond to this market demand.

There are, of course, a host of thoughtful, informative,
responsible news organizations and programs, just as there is
a lot of good music, movies, television and video games pro-

duced. But an increasing number of other news organizations are learning bad lessons from their cousins (or should I
now say parents) in the entertainment industry. The advent
of several all-news television channels, for instance, has increased the sources of information but also the competition
for audience. That has resulted in what Norman Ornstein,
one of the most astute observers of life in Washington, calls
the *"Crossfire-ization"* of our politics, in which confrontation
is required, screaming is encouraged and more heat than
light is generated. It is the news media's version of violent
programming, not quite *Natural Born Killers*, gangsta rap or
the World Wrestling Federation, but, on some news shows,
moving disturbingly closer.

Since Bob Woodward and Carl Bernstein won the
Pulitzer Prize for investigating and documenting the excesses and crimes of Watergate and helped to bring down the
Nixon presidency, a generation of journalists has focused on
exposing public wrongdoing as the path to success and
honor. This has created some very good deterrence against
bad behavior by public officials. But, more recently, for reasons that I suspect have a lot to do with increasing competition in the news business and lower standards in the
entertainment media, some news organizations have been
too quick to allege or suggest immorality or illegality before
it is confirmed, judging officials guilty until proven innocent
instead of the traditional other way around. This might be
called the scandalization of our politics.

The news media's *"Crossfire-ization"* of public life not
only undercuts the cooperation among elected officials that
is necessary for them to accomplish anything, but it also encourages political leaders to behave in ways that are most
likely to turn off the public, deepening its disengagement
from government. The same is true of the scandalization of

politics, which discourages good people from entering public life because they do not want to expose their lives to such investigation and attack. I am not blaming all of government's current shortcomings on the news media. The opposite is the case. Most of government's problems are self-created, but the news media, in their focus on the negative and encouragement of the nasty, make pre-existing governmental shortcomings much worse.

People in public life are themselves quite capable of using the airwaves—free or commercial—to attack each other in a way that has the exact same effect as the news media's *Crossfire*-ization: less internal cooperation and less external respect. Their motivation may also be unsettlingly similar. While some of the worst behavior of the entertainment industry and news media is motivated by a desire for higher ratings and larger quarterly income, some of the worst behavior of elected officials in raising campaign money and spending it attacking each other is motivated by a desire for higher poll numbers and more votes. Each of them— entertainment industry executives, news media producers, and elected officials and their political consultants—slides into conduct that is harmful to the long-term health of our country in pursuit of short-term gains for themselves, their corporations or their political parties.

The current deficiencies of these three central societal institutions—entertainment, news and government—therefore have a similar cause: the failure of the individuals who lead them to apply traditional community standards and interests to their work—standards that would reflect rather than reject America's core values and that would elevate rather than denigrate our government. Because our sense of ourselves as Americans is, to a significant extent, rooted in our attitude toward the institutions of our government, our nation's confidence and vitality are diminished whenever those government institutions become pawns in a political chess game or playthings in a news media ratings game.

The first evidence of the American spiritual awakening I believe is now happening occurred in the 1970s and particularly in the 1980s, in millions of private acts of revulsion with the loss of public morality by people who then looked to religion as the best way to rebuild that morality around themselves and their families. They returned to their churches, synagogues, mosques and temples and to many nontraditional spiritual movements for values, order and peace of mind. It was as if people were responding to the ancient plea of the prophet Hosea, "Thou hast stumbled in thine iniquity. . . . Therefore, turn thou to thy God [and] keep mercy and justice." Those separate, spontaneous acts began to express themselves politically in the emergence of the so-called Religious Right in the 1980s. Although it frightened many people with its mix of church and state, the Religious Right seems to me in hindsight to have been more right than not in its expressed concern about the decline of community morality and decay of our public culture. Then in their 1992 campaign and in the administration that followed, President Clinton and Vice President Gore embraced those moral concerns and made them the center of a broader, new political consensus. It was President Clinton who said "Americans feel that instead of celebrating their love for God in public, they're being forced to hide their faith behind closed doors. That's wrong." Clinton and Gore gave life to this new consensus in small but important ways (as in their support of school uniforms and the V-chip) and at moments of national trauma such as the Sunday after the federal building in Oklahoma City was bombed when President Clinton gave a speech to Oklahomans that was one of the finest expressions of America's civil religion—deistic, inclusive, purposeful and comforting—that has ever been given.

A different kind of evidence of political awakening came when the American people began to break out of the hesitancy that Alan Wolfe wrote about to reach public judgment about values. It happened most effectively in their condemnation of the welfare and criminal justice systems and the federal fiscal deficit. The people made clear to politicians that they saw these governmental programs and practices as corruptions of traditional American values of personal responsibility and examples of the anything-goes philosophy that was degrading our country. Although Republicans had long condemned the status quo in welfare and crime and the budget deficit, it is significant that it was the Democratic Clinton-Gore administration that responded to those condemnations and brought forth the anti-crime law of 1994, the welfare reform law of 1996 and the budget balancing acts of 1993 and 1997. A rising public chorus of value judgments had reached the leaders of *both* parties and led to a change in laws and practices that expressed those values and, incidentally, that worked. Crime rates are way down, welfare rolls have dropped by half and the federal government's budget is in surplus for the first time in a generation.

Because of the pivotal part President Clinton played in accelerating these early expressions of an American political awakening, it is ironic and sad that the President's relationship with Monica Lewinsky and the resulting impeachment process in 1998 and 1999 gave the awakening its next push forward, but first it brought our government, culture and nation to new lows. The Clinton-Lewinksy saga is the most vivid example we have of the virus of lost standards being passed back and forth among the entertainment culture, the news media and government, making each more ill. The nation's highest office became the stage on which a tawdry soap opera was acted out, broadcast, politicized, satirized and analyzed ad nauseam. The President's relationship with Ms. Lewinsky forced the American people, including those of us who serve in government, to confront the new realities of public life in America and the moral complexities that are at its heart. It required all of us to sort out conflicting values and sentiments which mirrored the traditional tensions I have spoken of between the individual's freedom and privacy and the community's need for values and standards. We had to reconcile our discomfort with the intrusiveness and negativism of the news media with our understanding that public officials are role models and therefore their conduct in both public and private matters to the community; to balance our respect for the presidency and our affection for this President with our anger and disgust about his behavior with Ms. Lewinsky.

The American people struggled very personally with these thoughts and feelings during the days of August 1998 after the President admitted that he had not told us the truth about his relationship with Ms. Lewinsky. In Connecticut, people wrote me, called me and stopped me at the supermarket or on the beach to share their conclusions or confusion, and to ask for my counsel or support. Some argued, as the President had, that his relationship with Ms. Lewinsky was private and should not affect the superb leadership he had given our country. Others were furious that his behavior had given their children a bad course in sex education and undercut the importance of telling the truth.

On September 3, 1998, I reached my own resolution of these conflicts when I went to the Senate Chamber and delivered what I described as "the most difficult statement I have made in my ten years in the Senate." I called the President's behavior "disgraceful," "immoral," "harmful" and "too consequential for us to walk away from." I took strong issue with the President's argument that his relationship with Ms. Lewinsky was "nobody's business" but his family's and that "even presidents have private lives."

"Whether he or we as a people think it is fair or not," I said, "the reality in 1998 is that a president's private life is public." When he misbehaves in private, he risks damaging the country he heads, compromising the trust of the people he serves and diminishing his capacity to lead. In our democracy, the question of how the news media are regulated is, under the First Amendment, thankfully up to them, not up to public officials. Therefore, until the media draw new, less intrusive lines around their news coverage, people in public life must assume that the most private aspects of their lives can, in an instant, become globally public. While we may regret this loss of privacy, it will often be good for our country because the private conduct of a public official can have real and serious effects on his or her ability to carry out governmental responsibilities, and therefore sunlight—even the harsh sunlight of the contemporary media—can, as Justice Brandeis once said, be a helpful and effective disinfectant. The greater the power a person holds in government, the greater is his or her responsibility to behave correctly because the worse are the effects of personal misbehavior on the government and the people he or she serves. That is certainly the lesson the Bible teaches in many places, including, poignantly, God's refusal to allow the great leader Moses to enter the Promised Land because of his single loss of faith and control when he struck the rock to get water. When a national leader makes himself vulnerable, he thereby makes his government and his people vulnerable.

Although the American people struggled with what the

President had done and how to react to it, they ultimately reached a clear judgment that his behavior was immoral and had hurt our country. But they distinguished that moral judgment from their political judgment, and concluded that under the Constitution the behavior the President had admitted to did not make him a danger to America or unable to continue to perform his duties, and therefore could not justify his removal from office. Everything I read about the history of the impeachment clauses led me to agree with them.

What is striking in hindsight is that the American people were not hesitant to assert publicly what they believed privately, which was that the President was wrong. In other words, these traumatic events forced them out of their moral silence and their reluctance to judge the behavior of others. They held the President accountable to community standards of morality. I see in this reaction further evidence that the current spiritual awakening is bringing forth a political awakening, which continues into the 2000 presidential election as the voters say over and over again that they want a president they can respect. They don't want anyone to confuse the political judgment of "not guilty" they made about impeachment with their moral judgment of "guilty" about the President's misconduct and its consequences. In the early presidential primary states of the 2000 election, there seems to be increased public interest and serious questioning of the candidates, as if people are coming to understand how much they and the country lose when they are disengaged from the political system and when their leaders act irresponsibly.

We who serve in government also learned lessons about the consequences of private misconduct on our public lives and on our constituents that should deter such misconduct for some time to come. But we also must realize that we can hasten the nascent American political and cultural awakening by acting in our private and public lives in a manner that respects America's best values—including civility—and therefore increases public confidence and trust in government. We must try to embrace and express those values in our governmental work by, for example, adopting more laws like welfare and criminal justice reform that incorporate them. We can help end the divisive partisanship that currently afflicts our government by tearing off those partisan uniforms and working across party lines for the common good. And when we do disagree, we can surely find words and ways to do so that are not divisive and demeaning.

There are limits, however, to what people in public life now can or will do to bring about the change we need. For the current awakening to truly become America's next great awakening, it must engage the public. When the American people work hard for a goal, they usually achieve it. And this is exactly what now needs to happen with our politics, culture and community life. The people—not just special interest groups, not just powerful businesses, not just big-money contributors, not just fringe elements, but the core of America that has remained on the sidelines as our cultural and political values have eroded—must make their voices heard in support of moral standards, drawing lines between right and wrong, acceptable and unacceptable behavior, particularly in the shared spaces of our public life.

There are some encouraging signs that those voices are beginning to speak out and be heard across the American landscape:

- In public places, including schools, where officials, citizens and students are finding constitutional ways to honor and express their religious faith; and in schools where "character education"

programs like Character Counts (some of them
federally funded), which teach the values of civility,
integrity, trustworthiness, tolerance, responsibility,
fairness, cooperation and citizenship, are increasingly being incorporated into classroom curricula;

• In the entertainment industry, where a
surge of persistent public pressure—a "revolt of the
revolted"—has prodded at least some executives in
the television and motion picture industries to acknowledge that they have civic responsibilities to a
society (especially to its children) that is strongly
influenced by their companies' programming and
to say they will work to stem the violent, perverse
and puerile content (the "avalanche of crud," as
film critic David Denby calls it) produced by their
companies—we need much more of this;

• And in the news media, where surveys show
that the public's level of faith, trust and respect for
the standards of journalism, which were so buoyed
in the wake of Woodward and Bernstein's work on
the Watergate scandal, have plunged since then,
hand in hand with the public's loss of trust in politicians. Recognizing that their industry has seen its
own standards slip, that the intensity of the rush to
capture readers and viewers in the highly competitive newspaper, magazine and television markets has
in too many cases compromised reporters' allegiance to accuracy and integrity, and realizing that
the hunt for scandal and controversy has increasingly pushed media investigations further into the
private lives of public figures than many American
people think is relevant, publishers, editors and

broadcast executives in newsrooms across America
have begun redrawing the lines for their reporters,
defining boundaries that reflect the public's need to
know and retightening the fundamental journalistic
standards of accuracy and fairness that have become
too loose during recent years.

Just as what has ailed our government, culture and news
organizations has spread from one to the other, so too can
the recovery of each help restore the well-being of the others. In none of these areas is morality being legislated. The
policy shifts and raising of standards taking place today are a
voluntary response to persistent pressure from the public,
from the American people themselves. It must continue and
grow stronger. People are also organizing in communities
across America to combat some of the worst effects of our
moral and cultural decay, like violent crime and teenage
pregnancy, and their efforts are succeeding, as some of the
most recent statistics have shown, with homicide rates and
teenage pregnancy dropping. Charitable contributions are
up, the young are turning to community service professions
in greater numbers and, either because the economy has
been booming or in spite of it, people are finding they need
more than material wealth to achieve happiness. They want
spiritual fulfillment, cultural inspiration, more time with
their families and more confidence that they are making a
difference for the better.

With all these encouraging signs of a spiritual and political awakening, now is truly the time when our country needs
more people to become active in public life. Not every
American can or should seek elective office, but every American can and should use his or her citizenship to make our

158 IN PRAISE OF PUBLIC LIFE

government better, to make it as good, in President Carter's phrase, as the American people are. And there is no secret as to how you can use your citizenship to elevate our public life:

- by registering to vote and voting;
- by contacting elected officials and stating your desires and beliefs on particular issues;
- by getting involved in campaigns for candidates who support your beliefs;
- by personally applying those beliefs through some form of public or civil service;
- and, ultimately, by running for public office yourself, if you desire.

If, for example, the dizzying and dismaying amount of money it takes to run for Congress or the presidency today seems outrageous and corrupting to you, as it does to me, demand that the rules for raising and spending money on political campaigns be reformed. The solutions to this problem are ultimately not mysterious or complicated. First, we must close the soft-money loophole, meaning that individuals, corporations and unions will be clearly and legally limited in how much money they can give a candidate or party. Second, we should require television and radio stations, as a public interest condition of their licenses, to give large amounts of free airtime to candidates before each election. Third, in return for the free airtime, the law should limit how much each candidate can spend in a campaign, based on how many voters are in the state or district where the candidate is running. And fourth, although we probably cannot constitutionally limit the amount of money special interest groups spend on issue advertisements during campaigns, we *can* do more to

make sure they are issue-focused and not candidate advertisements.

If these changes could be made, they would raise the
public's trust in government and thereby naturally improve
one of the most worrisome vital signs of our democracy
today—the dreadfully low and sinking rate of voter turnout.
It was 49.1 percent in 1996, the lowest in a presidential election year since 1924, and 36.1 percent in 1998, the lowest in
a nonpresidential year since 1942. It is time to make the raising of these rates of participation in our political system a
hard national goal. We should commit ourselves to targets:
as starters, 60 percent in presidential elections and 50 percent in nonpresidential years. To help achieve these goals, we
should change the laws of every state to make it legal for voters to register at the polls on election day, and we should ini-
tiate a very aggressive multi-media advertising campaign to
inspire, shame and badger more Americans to vote.

We who are in politics now can do more to encourage
people to vote by searching for ways to make the political
process more relevant to them, bringing the political parties
to where the people are—to schools, malls, workplaces and
play places. The Internet provides us with extraordinary new
opportunities to engage people in discussion of public issues.
Just as I started going to diners in Connecticut to meet the
average citizens who don't belong to special interest groups,
we now need to create "e-diners" to do the same.

If the American people rise up and get involved in their
government, they will diminish the disproportionate power
of the activated minorities—the special interest groups—that
has driven us toward the unhealthy polarization and partisanship of our government right now. An energized mainstream majority advocating shared values will embolden

elected officials to be as independent as their personal beliefs lead them to be or it will bring new people into positions of power. It will return our government to its founding ideals, and raise our country to its noblest aspirations. There is so much important work to be done: improving our schools, helping more people into the economic mainstream, protecting the environment, providing better health care, guaranteeing retirement security and keeping America secure and involved in a changing world.

H. L. Mencken, whose general cynicism about human nature would make him seem an unlikely spokesman for representative government, once wisely said that the cure to whatever ails democracy is more democracy. Teddy Roosevelt put the matter succinctly: "The government is us," he said. "We are the government. You and I." Only *we* can make it better.

The great T.R. added, in stirring words written more than a century ago that need to resonate in every American heart and head today:

It is not the man [or woman] who sits by his fireside reading his evening paper, and saying how bad our politics and politicians are, who will ever do anything to save us; it is the man [or woman] who goes out into the rough hurly-burly of the caucus, the primary, and the political meeting, and there faces his fellows on equal terms. The real service is rendered not by the critic who stands aloof from the contest, but by the man [or woman] who enters it and bears his part. . . .*

* *Theodore Roosevelt*, American Ideals *(New York: G. P. Putnam's Sons, 1920)*, p. 36.

We Americans are a blessed people living in the most free, prosperous and secure country in the history of the world. We have been given an unmatched legacy of national principle and purpose—freedom and opportunity—that will be lost unless it is nurtured and advanced by each succeeding generation. This generation of Americans must not, and will not, sit back in material comfort, moral impotence or personal apathy and let these enormously valuable national assets of citizenship slip away.

I said at the beginning that this would be a book with a point of view, a book in praise of public life. But it is also a plea, a fervent plea *for* public life, not just for its satisfaction, excitement and honor but for its necessity. American democracy and self-government are endangered today by the American people's retreat from their government and politics. Our country's future requires that they reengage—at least to vote, at best to serve.

The day is short, as that rabbi said so long ago, and there is much work to be done, *tikkun olam*, repairing our government and improving our beloved country and world. We are not required to complete the work ourselves, but, as good and grateful citizens, we cannot withdraw from it either.

ACKNOWLEDGMENTS

Writing this book was truly a labor of love because the case it aspires to make for the necessity, value and honor of public life is very dear to me. I am therefore deeply grateful to all the people who inspired or assisted me in this effort.

I must begin by thanking Alice Mayhew, vice president and editorial director at Simon & Schuster, who conceived of this book and gave me the opportunity to write it. Having now worked with Alice, I understand why she has such an extraordinary reputation and is such a towering presence in the world of publishing. She has made a difference.

I also thank Alice for pushing me past my pride as a writer of books and convincing me to accept the collaboration of Michael D'Orso on this work. It would not have ended as well as I hope it has, and certainly not as early, without Michael's assistance. He is a superb and disciplined writer, and, for me, was an inspiring muse and very helpful collaborator. Together, I hope we have achieved Alice's goal that this book be written more like a conversation with the reader than a Senate floor speech.

On Michael's behalf and mine, I thank his agent, David Black, and Simon & Schuster associate editor Ana DeBevoise for their efforts. I also thank my friend and attorney, Bob

Barnett, for wisely and ably guiding me through this project. My executive assistants in Washington and Hartford, Melissa Winter and Heather Picazio, deserve special thanks for their multi-faceted help and for finding the time for me in my schedule which enabled me to write this book.

For his encouragement and support, I am grateful to my childhood friend from Stamford, Connecticut, Jack Romanos, now president of Simon & Schuster. In Jack's case, this is nothing new. He has been supporting me since I first ran for president of our junior high school class.

For their insights and advice, I thank two friends, Bill Galston and Norman Ornstein, who are also two of America's best political thinkers.

As a state senator, attorney general and United States senator, I have been blessed with a most able and dedicated staff, without whom this journey would not have been productive or enjoyable. I thank them all and particularly want to mention Sherry L. Brown, who has been my campaign manager and state office director for almost two decades now; Laura Cahill, Joan Jacobs and Ken Dagliere, who have been leaders in my Hartford office; Michael Lewan and Bill Andresen, who have been, successively, my chiefs of staff in Washington; Bill Bonvillian, who has been my legislative director and public policy mentor in the Senate; Jim Kennedy, who was my communications director as attorney general and for the first eight years in the Senate, before he moved on to the White House; Eric Federing and Dan Gerstein, who succeeded Jim; Carleen Overstreet Morris, who was my executive assistant from 1989 until 1998, when she left to raise a family; Clarine Nardi Riddle, who was my deputy when I was attorney general; Brad Robideau of my Washington staff; and James K. O'Connell, my special assistant plenipotentiary for thirty years.

I can never adequately thank my family, who have always been the foundation of my life and work, but let me here express my love and gratitude to my mother and my father, of blessed memory; to all my uncles and aunts, especially my uncle Ben Manger for his steadfast support from my birth to his death in 1995; to my sisters, Rietta and Ellen, and their families; to my children, Matt and April, Rebecca, Ethan and Ariela, and Hani; to my grandchildren, Tennessee and Willie; and finally and ultimately, to my wife, Hadassah Freilich Lieberman, to whom I dedicate this book, for being my beloved partner, counsellor and friend.

JOSEPH I. LIEBERMAN
New Haven, Connecticut
October 1999

INDEX

socializing among members
of, 103
speaking fees earned while in,
77
status and, 104
weekly prayer breakfast for,
103
weekly schedule in, 113
work overload in, 93–95
Serbia, 129–30
Sheehy, Gail, 24
Silent Spring (Carson), 34
Silver, Thomas H., 13*n*
Simpson, Alan, 93–94, 95, 99
"size of the fee" rule, 49
slavery, 141
Slovenia, 129
Smith College, 62
"soft money," 122, 123–24, 158
Sosa, Sammy, 39
South, 33, 35
South Dakota, 81
Soviet Union, 130
special interest groups, 22, 54,
109–10, 111, 117–19,
158–59
Spouses of the Senate, 98
Springfield, Mass., 71
Squier, Bob, 80–81
Srebenica, 130
Stamford, Conn., 25, 26, 27–28,
68, 74, 91, 137
state governments, 43
Steiger, Paul, 33
Stevens, Ted and Cathy, 95
Stevenson, Adlai, 27, 30
suburbs, 27–28
Sullivan, Pat, 89
Supreme Court, U.S., 70

Tabor, Mary B. W., 15*n*
Talmud, 25
Tammany Hall, 49

Tamraz, Roger, 122–23
Tarfon, Rabbi, 25
television, 9–10, 26, 118, 147
cable franchises for, 49–50
Congressional coverage on,
110–11
political campaigning and,
43–44, 59, 73, 80, 82, 85,
87, 88–89, 123, 124
rating system for, 135–36
television industry, 84–85
Tennessee, 21
term limits, 20, 22
Texas, 96, 116
third parties, 40–41
Thomas, Clarence, 13
Thoreau, Henry David, 40
tikkun olam, 25, 32, 161
"time beyond time," 101
Tucker, Ethan, 66, 94
Tucker, Hadassah Freilich, *see*
Lieberman, Hadassah
Freilich Tucker
Twenty-seventh Psalm, 51

United Nations, 130
Utah, 133

values:
cultural, 135–36, 141–46
family, 79, 91
V-chip, 135, 150
Ventura, Jesse, 21, 40
Veterans Administration (VA),
136
Vicino, Bob, 57
victims' rights, 56
video games, 135, 146, 147
Vietnam War, 13, 51, 137
Village Voice, 80
violence, 139–40
Virginia, 129, 131
visas, 133–34

ABOUT THE AUTHORS

JOSEPH LIEBERMAN has represented Connecticut in the U.S. Senate since 1989. He is chairman of the Democratic Leadership Council, and is a member of the Armed Services, Environment and Public Works, Governmental Affairs and Small Business Committees. The author of four books, Lieberman lives with his wife, Hadassah, and their four children in New Haven and in Washington, D.C.

MICHAEL D'ORSO is the author of *Rosewood: Like Judgment Day* and the co-author of *Walking with the Wind: A Memoir of the Movement*, with U.S. Congressman John Lewis of Georgia. D'Orso lives in Norfolk, Virginia.